BEAT THE BOTS

Judy

To my best
cheerleader!
Thank you
for helping me
get here!

BEAT
THE
BOTS

HOW YOUR HUMANITY
CAN FUTURE-PROOF YOUR
TECH SALES CAREER

ANITA NIELSEN

LIONCREST
PUBLISHING

BEAT THE BOTS
How Your Humanity Can Future-Proof Your Tech Sales Career

ISBN   978-1-5445-0345-5   *Hardcover*
       978-1-5445-0344-8   *Paperback*
       978-1-5445-0346-2   *Ebook*

Cover design by Marissa Rogers
Book design by John van der Woude

*For Gurdev & Chanchala Dhawan, my dad & mom,
with respect and gratitude for patiently guiding me as I
created my own unique path to joy and success, and for
your blessings and support every step of my way.*

*For my remarkable children, Niyam & Navin for paying
attention every time I remind you to make good choices and
that the elephant always, always wins. It's a wonder to watch
and cheer each of you on every day as you search for the
stones that will help you pave your paths to fulfillment.*

*For my brand-new nephew and niece, Aiven Dev &
Amal Pyari Dhawan, with blessings and great hope that
you'll always hold dear the values and principles your
grandparents brought with them when they came to the
United States. As you grow and shape your own paths
to happiness, I promise these will be your best guide.*

CONTENTS

PREFACE

Let me tell you about Neil.

Neil is a 42-year-old B2B technology sales professional at a mid-size technology products and services company. He is super-likable, has a great sense of humor, and has always been exceptional at creating customer business relationships.

When I met Neil, he had recently lost a couple of landmark deals with existing customers. He was disappointed and a little depressed that even his long-standing, seemingly strong relationships weren't enough to protect him from losing customers to the competition or to the dreaded "do nothing" decision. He knew that what he sold wasn't differentiated. There were countless other companies offering the same technology and similar services. He also found it was getting more difficult to know what customers valued or what that "winning play" could be for a customer. None of the things he had been trained on could consistently address the various types of buyers he met.

Forget "one size fits all"—none of the haphazard training he'd received even got close to "one size fits most."

Neil knew he had to sharpen his skills and find a way to stand out. His company didn't really invest much in helping him learn and grow. Sure, they had some training sessions over the years but those just covered whatever training buzz or book the CEO had bought into that quarter. He didn't have the time and energy to sort through all the training tools and methodologies to figure out what would work best for *him*. Neil wanted to stay current on sales as a discipline and new ideas that could help him—but he just couldn't, it really was all too much.

I learned he was under overwhelming pressure to provide well for his family, short and long term. A few years ago, his wife had given up her teaching career in order to stay at home with their two small children. This meant Neil was the sole earner for his family. Financially, that had always been an easy choice because Neil was consistently a top performing rep with commission checks reflecting that. He felt he would be a complete failure if he had to ask his wife to start working again, to help maintain their lifestyle and financial security. My heart hurt for Neil. He was just so down. I had to find a way to get him past this.

His boss was increasingly disappointed with him and the daily pressure was excruciatingly high. He just was not making the kind of money needed to sustain his family's lifestyle. As a sales professional, husband and father, these challenges were direct threats to his self-confidence. Diminished self-confidence impedes the ability to be resilient in facing the day-to-day rejections that are a normal part of a sales career.

Above and beyond all of these things—adding insult to injury—Neil was afraid (rightfully so) that B2B sales professionals were rapidly becoming irrelevant, and going to be rendered obsolete sooner rather than later. Articles he had read that told him about how B2B salespeople are "dead" or are "dying" were just mortifying (hah—see what I did there?). When he thought about it, there were actually a lot of things he did that could be automated or be taken over by robots. Hell, Amazon and CDW were already leading his customers to go out and buy their equipment on their own via their respective websites.

Neil found himself feeling a bit desperate. Desperation tends to make for bad choices. Neil had been having difficulty with qualifying opportunities because his fear and desperation prevented him from walking away from any deal. He felt he just couldn't afford to. Additionally, working on poorly qualified deals was taking time from his existing customer accounts. These accounts were losing confidence in Neil's ability to be responsive and meet their needs, leaving him vulnerable to competition preying on these customers. The snowball just kept rolling downhill, gathering speed.

Does any of this sound familiar? If you picked up this book, I have a feeling it may.

Over the years, I have met hundreds of amazing sales professionals in situations similar to Neil's, trying to figure out a way to differentiate themselves from competing forces—which, today, means things like AI, automation, and robots (bots, as I like to call them—it just sounds more evil, right?).

When sales professionals come to me with obstacles like the ones Neil faced, some wacky empathy sensor in my brain goes haywire. I feel an overwhelming desire to help them get through it. I've stopped questioning why this happens; I'm just going with it and loving every minute because of Neil and all the extraordinary sales professionals I meet along the way.

INTRODUCTION

Slimy. Sneaky. Shady.

Why does the word "salesperson" conjure up such derogatory adjectives in most people's minds?

I get that, once upon a time, the vast majority of salespeople weren't compelled to be completely honest, and therefore were able to get away with some questionable behavior. You can probably picture this type of old-school salesperson—maybe at a used car dealership, wearing an awful 1970s-style plaid sport coat, the requisite gold neck chain gleaming under the fluorescent lights.

Let's call him Leisure Suit Larry. (If you get that reference, high five, fellow child of the 80s!)

In pretty much every old-school sales scenario, Larry smooth-talks an unsuspecting buyer to get them to purchase a car that is just short of being labeled a lemon. But if I think about it, I haven't seen Larry, or anyone like him, anywhere in at least a decade. Have you? Can you imagine someone operating that way when every person who comes into the dealership can, within seconds of the first sign of shade or sneak, submit a scathing review to Yelp or to one of a dozen online car buyer forums? Customers can tweet a tirade about inauthenticity and dishonesty and the retweets could very well put that dealership out of business.

That's just the start. The power of social media seems to be endless—for better or for worse. Do you think a sleazy salesperson, in a dealership or anywhere else, stands a chance of surviving for very long in today's super-social society? I sure don't. Those days are gone.

It genuinely hurts my feelings to hear people continue to speak so negatively about sales professionals, as though they're all carrying on Larry's legacy. This is a natural reaction, given my career in B2B technology sales consulting and coaching. I've worked with hundreds of B2B technology sales professionals in companies large, small, and every size in between. I know how dedicated, talented, and service-minded the majority of them truly are. I've met maybe three Leisure Suit Larry types (ew) along the way, and I won't lie to you: a small part of me has enjoyed watching them learn the hard way that their approach isn't going to cut it in today's world.

The scary thing for me now is that other, more reputable B2B sales professionals may face a fate similar to Larry if they don't evolve their way of thinking and choose to change their approach.

THE RISE OF THE MACHINES

Over the past couple of years in the sales training and enablement industry, we've been spooked by industry guru reports talking about the "death" of the B2B salesperson, or predictions that 20 percent of sales professionals will be out of a job by 2020.[1] Not only that, but now we fear "The Rise of the Robot," that Artificial Intelligence (AI) will replace B2B sellers entirely.[2] It's a scary time for B2B sales professionals.

If this all sounds like nervous hand-wringing, make no mistake: robots and AI really *are* a threat. The oncoming

---

1   "Death Of A (B2B) Salesman". Forrester. April 13, 2015. https://www.forrester.com/report/Death+Of+A+B2B+Salesman/-/E-RES122288#
2   Martin Ford. *The Rise of the Robots. Basic Books. May 2015.*

AI revolution poses a significant threat to both your career and your bank balance.

As B2B technology sales professionals, you already know this, because you sell technology. You understand that automation can render well-worn resources obsolete and often cause people to lose their jobs. You are probably seeing the writing on the wall. Though you may not have been threatened by a robot or AI yet, it's just a matter of time.

The fact is, any savvy IT leader who wants to buy servers or other technology products and equipment doesn't have to call you anymore. He can go to any number of websites—CDW and Amazon, for example—to order technology equipment and services. There's likely even an option to add "installation services" to the online shopping cart. Once the purchase is made, someone contacts the customer and schedules the install. It's a pretty low-friction process, today. In these online purchasing scenarios, the IT buyer won't have to schedule a series of meetings, navigate a proposal, or endure any lengthy contract review or implementation process. And he'll probably save his company money by buying from a larger company that can offer him a lower price.

It's only going to get easier from here. Before we know it, everyone is going to be worried about losing a deal to

Amazon. If you're selling any type of technology, if it's not already on Amazon, it will be soon. If your customer can just go online and buy it themselves, why wouldn't they? Why would they bother to call you and have to work through a more complex process with a B2B tech sales person and their respective organization?

This. Is. Scary.

As someone that helps B2B sales professionals become invaluable to their buyers and future-proof their careers, the idea of B2B sales professionals being "dead" frustrates me. The truth is, B2B sales professionals are not only alive and kicking, but the best ones are seeing even greater success by choosing to learn, grow, and evolve. They know that this growth is crucial in order to compete with machines. They also know that, although it is becoming increasingly difficult to differentiate in transactional sales, the opportunity to differentiate in complex sales has actually increased. The top B2B sales professionals are already preparing to beat the bots and stay ahead of AI.

My career began in the B2B technology sales industry; I've always been drawn to B2B tech sales. I think it's because the various layers of complexity allow me to think strategically and problem-solve. At the end of the day, that's what any successful B2B sales professional does, too; to effectively sell technology to a business, you have to know the technology inside and out, and be an expert in the ways a specific customer can apply that tech to achieve their company's goals. This type of sale requires a much deeper understanding of a buyer's business needs and challenges. So, even with the "rise of the machines," long-term success in a B2B tech sales career depends on your ability to focus on the exact opposite of technology's value; you have to master human value.

Okay, Anita, but...WTF does that even mean?

Let me explain. Mastering human value begins with understanding that the only thing that truly, consistently matters when it comes to winning B2B tech sales, or any sale, is the value created through the human-to-human interaction between seller and buyer. In other words, true value stems from a salesperson taking the time to understand what matters most to their client and finding unique ways to create that value.

This is human-to-human, H2H, selling, not just B2B. B2B sales is all about creating and articulating value and, typically, whoever does this best wins the deal. The value in H2H selling is truly differentiated, distinct by its very nature, because an individual sales rep creates it specifically for his/her buyer. H2H sales professionals are empathetic and know to personalize value based on a thorough understanding of what value means to that customer and a sincere desire to help that person succeed.

You know what? *Robots can't do this.*

AI can't do what the best B2B sales professionals do. That will not change in our lifetime, if at all. As long as sales professionals can choose to shift their thinking and create ways to generate personalized value for the buyers they serve, robots or AI can't beat them. When a sales professional delivers personalized, H2H value, customers won't want to buy from machines.

This book will help you understand how to adapt to any sales context by using a thought process based on H2H interactions and human psychology. I'll teach you a way of thinking and some ideas that will help ensure that—as long as humans are doing the buying—robots can never outsell you.

THE H2H SALES EVOLUTION

At the risk of getting dangerously close to revealing my age, I'll tell you that I've been in sales or sales support for more than two decades (don't even start doing the math in your head). Very early on, I came to the realization that I'm *really* good as a direct sales rep. I consistently exceeded my targets and made a lot of money. I was doing well enough that I was often asked to help coach others on the team and help them learn to do the things that were working so well for me. I loved it.

I did not love, however, always feeling so much pressure, and not having a consistent, steady income. Even though I was doing well, I always felt like the tide could turn and I'd suddenly be unable to meet my financial goals. Honestly, I struggle with this even today as a successful business owner. Coupled with this is the fact that my dad was a first-generation Indian immigrant who worked two jobs for decades to ensure that our family was always financially secure. The importance of financial security is embedded deeply in my psyche.

In my career, nothing makes me happier than helping someone see just how good they can be. Realizing this led me to leave my role in direct sales and take on a leadership role in sales support. In these support roles, I did sales training, developed content and collateral, worked on large deals in support of top sales professionals, and several other forms of coaching for high potential sales reps.

Sort of an "embedded coach," if you will. But I soon ran up against the limitations of working for other companies; I was unable to personalize information in a way that customers understood and valued. Delivering someone else's message—especially since, sometimes, it wasn't in the customer's best interest—wasn't an option for me if I wanted to be able to sleep at night.

I decided that in order for me to be successful and happy, I needed to go out on my own as an independent consultant focused on growing sales professionals and solving challenges within sales organizations. At least I would never have to do anything that I knew wasn't in the best interest of my client.

The one thing I know for sure about sales is that if the client doesn't trust that you have their best interests at heart, they won't buy from you. As a "solopreneur," I'm able to take the time to really understand my customer—both the individuals and the organizations. Then, I am able to provide the best guidance and direction for them, in the context of their business.

Anything short of that isn't happening on my watch.

DIFFERENTIATE YOURSELF
WITH TRUE VALUE

I asked a few of my clients, including sales leaders and individual sales professionals, to complete an anonymous survey. I asked them to explain to me why they choose to work with me. Overwhelmingly, the response to that question was along the lines of "I know you have my back" or "I know you will do whatever it takes to make me look good" and "no one else will care as much about what I need than you." I am humbled just knowing they completely trust that I have their best interests at heart. This is why I've been blessed enough to run a healthy business that, to date, is completely based on word-of-mouth and referrals.

I want the same thing for you. I want you to get so good at what you do that prospects will seek you out because of what they have heard from your customers. I want you to differentiate yourself to the point that prospects and customers simply won't consider buying from anyone else—robot, AI, competitor or otherwise.

I don't see sales professionals as a quota number to be achieved. I see you as very real, hard-working people who are trying to live the best life you can and, as humans are apt to do, want to meet or exceed your potential while on this planet (and maybe have some fun while doing it!).

Most of my interactions with sales professionals get unapologetically raw and human-to-human very quickly. Vulnerability happens. These are people who want to be the best they can be and, as an educator and lover of learning, I so admire that. I instinctively take on their plight as my own. Together, we find ways to focus on what matters most—the humanity of it all.

The human aspects of any sales interaction and the meaning that comes from them can't be commoditized. These parts are based on who you are, what you stand for, and what you determine is the most valuable way to help your customer. In other words, I teach people how to take who they are and what they stand for and use it to create something that is irresistible and invaluable to buyers.

I've been in the trenches alone and working big and small deals with sales professionals of all skill sets. I know how hard it is and all the things you do that managers and bean counters fail to see. I will share with you a thought process and behaviors that will lead you to win better, win bigger, and win more. Not only that, but if, like my beloved sales professional clients over the years, you implement what I teach you in this book, you'll find yourself at a point where your customers simply won't want to buy from anyone else. They will be loyal and they will help you to find more customers.

Here's what I believe: as long as humans are doing the buying, robots can't outsell you if you learn and apply the concepts you're about to read.

Some of you may not feel like you need the information I am talking about. You may think you're *that* good—that you're never going to be replaced by technology. If that's the case...well, we'll find out in a few years if you were right! Bye, and happy selling!

However, my experience tells me that every single one of you needs this book. You wouldn't have picked it up if you weren't the kind of sales professional that wants to grow and evolve; you get that you have nothing to lose by learning how to be better at your craft. Quite the opposite, in fact—you have everything to gain.

This book shows you how you can beat the bots and enjoy a fulfilling and successful B2B sales career for many, many years to come. So, keep reading; together, we'll make sure to keep the robots' hands off your career and your commission checks!

CHAPTER 1

VALUE IS IN THE EYE OF THE CUSTOMER

*If your customer does not perceive it as
value, then it's not really valuable.*

—Jeffrey Gitomer

A few years ago, I was coaching Ted, a B2B tech sales representative trying to sell a cloud-computing solution to a new prospect. He had been able to line up an appointment with the right people. I'd be joining him, and we worked together to prep. I stressed the importance of asking questions to discover what the customer really values.

FOOT IN MOUTH

The best and worst parts of being an embedded sales coach are that you see firsthand how your clients apply your training. Ted's meeting was the first one I'd ever joined him on. It seemed to start off fine. He asked some questions, a couple of open-ended ones, and the customer gave brief answers.

However, the customer's short answers made Ted nervous. He started going on about his company's cloud technology and how everyone was now looking at cloud solutions. A compelling benefit of a cloud solution was that it enabled his customers to shift from a capex (capital expenditure) to an opex (operating expenditure) model. He went on about how this made expenses more predictable, projections more accurate, and permitted his customers to get rid of aging tech equipment that took more effort to maintain and would inevitably break down. He was doing a great job of articulating what he had been trained to say about his cloud offering's features and benefits. It was clear he had learned all this really well.

As soon as Ted ended his speech, the prospect, clearly annoyed, said, "We don't prefer opex at all. We need to make capital expenditures in fixed assets because of the tax advantages of asset depreciation. That's not going to change."

Oh, shit.

The look on Ted's face was painful. He pretty much froze. After a few awkward seconds, I jumped in to try to turn the situation around. "That's interesting. We actually don't hear that often," I said. "How do you maintain your aging infrastructure?" I was trying to make it seem reasonable for Ted not to have known that a customer might prefer capital to operating expenditures.

Shifting the conversation got us back on track. I gave Ted "the Anita look," a non-verbal mix of "wtf?" "How many times have we been through this?" and "Seriously?" As you can imagine, his ride back to the office with me wasn't much fun.

It's not enough to tell customers how you have helped other customers. That can help build credibility, but, ultimately, customers want to know how you can help *them*.

SALES-TRAINING MISTAKES

You need to look at the world from your customer's perspective, and to do that, you've got to take the time to really understand that specific customer. Do thorough research before walking into a client meeting. Then, ask questions—lots of them. Curiosity is crucial in high-performance B2B technology sales. Ted learned this lesson the hard way, which is why he was left with his foot in his mouth.

Ted's nerves sent him down the wrong path. Getting short, seemingly abrupt answers made him nervous, and the conversation feel forced and awkward.

Ted then reached for the biggest crutch of all: his PowerPoint pitch deck. Ugh! The first bullet on the "Cloud Value" slide read "Capex to Opex." Ted looked at the bullet point and decided to discuss it in depth and at length. "Implementing a cloud solution enables a shift from capex to opex that many customers find valuable." Unfortunately, it was anything but valuable to the customer we were meeting with.

Rather than pulling out his slides, Ted should have remained calm and moved on to open-ended questions that would have helped him learn more about the customer's current business and technology needs. Ted needed to find out how cloud technology might matter to this specific prospect's business before pulling out generic pitch slides.

Unfortunately, a lot of B2B sales training sets reps up for this type of embarrassment. Their companies train them to make a pitch by spouting off generic value points for a given technology or service. I'm not saying reps shouldn't know what these are. They absolutely must. But this is only one take on the product or service. In this book, you'll learn to sit on the bullet points for a few minutes, so you can ask questions and understand what your customer finds relevant and valuable.

HUMAN-TO-HUMAN PERSONALIZATION

The Internet has changed everything in b2b sales. Buyers have changed the way they buy, so we have to change the way we sell. If a buyer does not have a clear picture of your value proposition, they won't buy from you. They have access to many other options that are easier, faster, and possibly cheaper, just a mouse-click away.

Innovations in business-to-consumer (b2c) sales are now coloring b2b buyer expectations. The most important shift is personalization. I estimate that about 15 percent of the items I buy on Amazon are a result of their recommendations. I don't need or look for these products, but when they show up on my home screen, I find I really like them. I like them enough to buy them, despite not needing them.

That's personalization. People today expect personalization in every aspect of buying and selling. They demand transparency and instant gratification. They're constantly engaging with websites that learn more and more about them with every purchase they make.

As author Daniel Pink says, we've moved from a "buyer beware" to a "seller beware" economy. You have to be prepared to make yourself matter to a customer, because there are so many other buying options. Some people even buy cars online! It sounds scary, but is it, really? If I am willing to buy every other product I need or don't need on Amazon, why wouldn't I buy a car online?

How can you adapt to these changes? How can you deliver value to a customer that is markedly more personalized than anything possible on a website? The only way to do so is to go H2H: human-to-human, bringing connection and personalization to every possible aspect of a sale.

This is how high performers instinctively sell. They make a B2B sale an H2H experience. They sell their own unique value, using what makes them human—their empathy and emotional intelligence (EI)—to sell to other human beings with their own unique emotions, ideas, and preferences. They take the time to thoroughly discover what matters to

the person on the other side of the table. They're personalizing in a way that websites, bots, and AI won't be able to,
at least not in most of our lifetimes.

Personalization is key when a sale is complex. You might
sell a few telecommunication systems or servers without
much personalization because these are straightforward
fulfillment sales of commodities. However, mastering personalization will consistently differentiate you in the sale
of a complex solution.

Equipment or plug-and-play-system sales are what bots,
AI, and Amazon will kill first. Sales professionals engaged
in these "transactional" situations are quickly learning that
their relationships won't protect them from losing business to websites or other competitors.

One of my clients, Jim, learned this the hard way. Jim
said he didn't have time for the coaching I was offering
through his workplace. I was okay with that. I don't allow
my clients to force my services on sales professionals.
There is no point in trying to help people who don't want
to be helped.

Then, Jim started to see his business dwindle. In the past,
he had a steady stream of orders from regular customers.

He never really had to work that hard because renewals and new orders from existing clients made life easy for him.

Jim started noticing orders decreasing. More and more frequently, customers would put business out for competitive bids, instead of just calling him to place an order. Competitors were now vying for his customers' business. Jim knew he had to show customers how the technology he was selling directly impacted their business needs. He had to learn to create value by differentiating his offerings.

All of a sudden, Jim wanted to sign up for coaching. We worked together on his ability to uncover and articulate value. A few weeks into our sessions, Jim had an "a-ha" moment. He had a particularly challenging deal with a customer, Matt, who did not value the relationship Jim had cemented with several others in his company. Jim and I worked to learn more about Matt from his peers at the company and through various social media platforms. We were able to figure out some things that were valuable to Matt, and Jim addressed them in various ways over the course of a few meetings with him.

Jim personalized his messaging in a manner that showed Matt he genuinely cared about his success and that he would do whatever it took to help him achieve his stated goals. The competitor hadn't even come close in this regard.

Matt ended up making his buying decision in Jim's favor. One of the original customer contacts at that company, with whom Jim had a long-standing relationship, reached out to Jim shortly after the deal was done.

Apparently, Matt had told him: "I can understand why you and the team don't want me to buy from the other company."

Hearing that made for a powerful "a-ha" moment for Jim. It helped him to completely transform the way he sells. I can tell you that Jim is tremendously successful now; he put in the effort to learn how to differentiate himself with personalized value, and it continues to pay off today.

To understand value, never assume what is important to a customer. You have to do due diligence and learn that from them. Ted could have completely changed the conversation with his client had he kept learning about them, rather than giving up because they weren't engaging much with his first few questions. Most of his questions were closed-ended to begin with, so it was already a stretch for him to expect more than one-word answers. Had he first focused on learning about the customer, he could have easily ascertained their views on capex and opex. I wouldn't have had to go into damage-control mode while Ted extracted his foot from his mouth.

LANDING THE BIG DEAL

One of Ted's colleagues, Tom, consistently and beautifully managed to do everything Ted should have done. Tom was my superstar. He made the time to gracefully ask as many questions as needed to understand his customers' perspectives. During one of my ride-alongs with him, he said something like this to a prospect:

"First off, I have to say, 'cloud' has become a buzzword. It's almost like it means so many different things that it actually doesn't mean much of anything. What I've learned is that it's important for me to understand what cloud specifically means to each of my customers. That's the only way I can help guide them to the best solution. So, would you mind telling me what 'cloud' means to you?"

Big, fat gold star for Tom! Up went the floodgates, and the customer kept sharing more and more information that we knew we could spin into gold.

First, Tom was transparent, showing he realized "cloud" had become something of a buzzword at this point. This neutralized any outright skepticism the customer might have had about the overuse of the term. It showed the customer that Tom cared enough to want to understand their viewpoint, which created rapport.

Then, Tom didn't say anything that made him seem like a know-it-all. He didn't break into pitch mode. He was telling the customer, "What matters to me is what this means to you," which is an incredibly powerful strategy. Not only did it give the customer the opportunity to speak—and people love to talk about themselves—but it also gave Tom the right to ask increasingly detailed questions.

Tom listened carefully throughout the meeting and responded in ways that tied directly to what the customer said. He never went into a pitch or a list of features and benefits. This is the first step in personalization, it creates trust and credibility. The customer naturally wanted to work with Tom. In fact, the prospect signed the third-largest deal in Tom's company's history, a multi-million-dollar contract with a five-year term. Just think how big Tom's commission check was.

During that legendary call, Tom got what has become known, a bit snarkily, as "Anita's gold star" look, one that says, "My baby's all grown up" and "I'm so proud, I'm about to cry." One of the "perks" of being an embedded coach is that you start to become a caricature.

Through years of being on countless initial prospect meetings, I have found that the high performers, the ones I know will outshine the bots, are experts at:

1. Making the conversation all about the customer or prospect;
2. Using thoughtful, open-ended questions to get customers talking about themselves; and
3. Paying close attention to the customer's every word, so there is no doubt that she knows she is being heard.

Top performers realize it is crucial to their success to understand what value means to each unique customer. They don't make assumptions based on their company's product and technology training, or about a customer's perception of value.

How well you understand what value means to your customer will make or break your deals. Sales is the discovery, creation, and exchange of value: value matters most.

YOUR KEY TAKEAWAY

What is valuable to you, and what your company has told you about your technology's value proposition, are not absolutes. Most of the time, such generic information will not create a perception of value that will differentiate you or motivate your customer to sign on the dotted line. You have to learn what value looks like to your customer. That's the only perspective that matters if you want to win bigger, better, and more. By the way, learning what is valuable to your customer before you start spewing what you think that is will help you keep your foot out of your mouth.

CHAPTER 2

VALUE MATTERS MOST

Care enough to create value for your customers.
If you get that part right, selling is easy.

—Anthony Iannarino

L et me make it real. I'm going to tell you a story of two sales reps working at an IT infrastructure solutions and services company—let's call it BigSib—and their customer, a global plastic-products manufacturer we'll call Alpha Corp.

POSITIONING

The first sales professional, Jennifer, had owned the Alpha Corp account for several years. Every time her company launched a new product, she'd tell the customer about it. Anytime the client had a relevant problem, she'd address it.

Jennifer did a good job selling products like servers and storage. Alpha Corp had used BigSib on a few projects, but nothing high-profile or high-impact. Jennifer often played golf with her Alpha Corp customers, especially the IT Director and his direct reports. She took them all out to a fancy steak dinner every quarter. She had established a healthy, if not particularly exceptional, relationship with them.

Jennifer's company wanted her to take the relationship to the next level and "maximize wallet share." Jennifer was being pressured to position BigSib's managed IT infrastructure services to Alpha Corp. This meant the customer giving BigSib remote control and management of all their servers and entire network; this then would generate a great deal more revenue.

Jennifer had mainly done transactional selling at Alpha Corp and had never gone deeper or higher in the organization than the IT department. She believed she'd risk losing her current relationships if she bypassed IT and went to the higher-ups. She was also afraid that if she tried to sell managed services—essentially IT outsourcing—her contacts would be done with her and start buying from a competitor that was dying to get the Alpha Corp account. This threat was very real. When you talk with IT leaders about outsourcing, they immediately assume you want to take their and their team's jobs away.

In the meantime, Jennifer found a great job at another company and left BigSib. Conventional wisdom says this is a big problem. The fear is that, if a sales rep leaves a company, it may lose one or more of the rep's customers. Jennifer and the Alpha Corp IT team had a good relationship. Wouldn't they just follow her to her new company? Maybe. Maybe not.

BigSib divided up Jennifer's accounts and gave Alpha Corp to another rep named Bill. Bill had been with BigSib for a while, although Alpha Corp and its industry were new to him. He researched Alpha Corp and set up a meeting with Jennifer's contacts. I was pulled in to join him at the meeting to help ensure things went smoothly. (I sometimes play the role of Linus's blanket.)

Since Bill was new to the account, he could ask a lot of questions without it seeming odd, and he did this well. He first showed that he understood the basics of the account, and then asked, "Who is responsible for your IT strategy?"

The Alpha Corp IT leader answered that this was the CIO who happened to be new to the company. Bill asked if things had changed since the new CIO had taken the helm. The floodgates suddenly lifted. The IT leader started talking and eventually revealed that the new CIO had been putting more pressure on the IT team to identify opportunities to innovate, but that no one actually knew what "innovate" meant.

Seeing an opportunity—or perhaps hearing a big CHA-CHING in his head—Bill suggested, "Why don't you and I meet with him and talk about this? I'm new, and that's a good reason to ask questions about what he means by 'innovate.' We may find out there's a way that BigSib can help you implement his ideas."

Bill did not simply ask for an introduction to the CIO, which is what some inexperienced salespeople might have done. How Bill positioned the CIO meeting with the IT Director is what made it happen. The IT leader would learn something he needed to know to succeed, meaning the meeting would also benefit him. By asking the right questions, Bill figured out that getting introduced to the new CIO would be valuable to the IT Director—and was it ever!

Over the course of two meetings, Bill found out that the new CIO was struggling with the best ways of using innovative technology to benefit the business. He wanted to look good to the executive team that had taken a chance by bringing him into Alpha Corp. Bill also knew that the IT team didn't have the time to learn about the innovations that would benefit the business, because they were inundated with operations and delivering services. Neither the CIO nor IT leader knew that BigSib could take over all their day-to-day infrastructure management. Jennifer, not wanting to jeopardize her relationship with the IT director by positioning "outsourced" services, had never told them.

Bill sold the managed-services solution and made the CIO and IT leader customers for life. He knew both of them highly valued looking good to their respective bosses.

Bill positioned BigSib's IT solution in a way that showed Alpha Corp they could achieve their goals within their organization. He completely changed the way the customer perceived BigSib: as a service partner rather than just a product vendor. Bill took the relationship far beyond where Jennifer had ever taken it, by first understanding what was valuable to both the IT director and the CIO, and *then* identifying how BigSib could deliver that value. The customer also knew they would benefit from Bill's ongoing personal guidance, which was a big reason why they signed the deal in the first place.

TYPES OF VALUE

Is "value" starting to feel like a buzzword to you? Are you feeling like we should play a drinking game with a shot for each time I use "value"? (Don't do that. It will get ugly, fast.) I know we've been talking about value a lot, and maybe it's starting to feel nebulous.

So, let's drill down into the meaning of value by breaking it into three layers or types that move from undifferentiated to highly differentiated. General value is the least differentiated, followed by Company value, then Personalized value, which is the most differentiated. Looking at value in this way helps you become a "purveyor of value," knowing you have to identify and articulate it at each of these levels. How you choose to create and highlight value to your customers determines your sales performance. The value you uncover, create, and position in your customer interactions is the most critical component of sales.

GENERAL VALUE

General value is your product, technology, or solution's inherent value. It's why the product was developed in the first place. For example, a toothbrush's general value is that it cleans teeth. For the purposes of this book, general value is a technology product, service, or solution's basic or obvious purpose. It's directly tied to your customer's need and is the value that results from addressing that need.

For instance, every b2b cloud solutions seller has to know why cloud computing or servers are valuable to their customers. General value is inherent in the technology, regardless of who the manufacturer is or the product's name. As a seller, you must understand that general value is not something you can control, influence, or use as a differentiator.

Articulating a product or solution's general value is table stakes. In other words, aside from knowing what it is, there's not much more that you can or need to do with general value. It gets you in the door. Recognizing its general value, customers know they want to buy a product to address a need. Sometimes, you don't even need to bring the subject up, because general value is simply assumed and expected.

General value is kinda like the "duh" part of the value story.

Examples of products' general value are:

- Telecommunications Solution → Greater collaboration, improved communication, increased productivity
- Cloud Computing → Scalability, flexibility, speed to market
- IT Network Solutions → Increased speed and efficiency, enhanced user and customer experience

Customers almost always know what the general value is of whatever you are selling. It's the reason they are asking about the product or technology in the first place. They need the outcomes it inherently delivers.

COMPANY VALUE

The next layer is company value, the value a company adds to the general value inherent in a product or solution. This is the value that, in theory, only your company is able to offer. Perhaps it's an additional warranty, award-winning customer care or an enhanced service agreement. Company value is how a specific vendor puts its own mark on a product or service's general value. For example, a telecommunications company might add tailored adoption services, such as end-user training. This added value helps a company differentiate itself from competitors.

However, company value is often only a differentiator up to a point. Given the competitive nature of business technology sales, it's usually only a matter of time before another company matches your company's "value-add." When this happens, company value becomes general value: something expected and not a point of differentiation. As a technology sales professional, you can't really influence or control if and when this happens.

Company value can be used as a differentiator until customers realize other companies are now doing what yours does. At that point, you can no longer shout "look at our added value" from the rooftops. If you did, you'd probably get a big fat "yours and everybody else's" in response.

PERSONALIZED VALUE

Here we are at last: personalized value, the concept that is the foundation of this book and everything I preach and teach. Personalized value is the only type of value entirely created by you, the sales professional. It is the value resulting from your deep understanding of the buyer's needs and keen insight into what will make that buyer succeed. Because personalized value is based on human interaction, it cannot be copied and is completely differentiated. No one else can create and deliver your brand of personalized value to your customer. Only you can. Personalized value is what will ensure you'll beat the bots every time, and that you'll enjoy a successful sales career for many years to come.

Sadly, most B2B tech sales professionals don't reach the personalized-value layer. They don't make the time to really understand not just buyers' technology needs, but also their personal and professional needs. Sales leaders who bring me in to help their sales teams almost always mention "the secret sauce." They want to know what the "secret sauce" is: what enables their top performers to win so much more than their mid-level reps? I don't fully buy in to the idea of a "secret sauce," but I can tell you that bottling up the ability to consistently deliver personalized value will get you pretty close.

This is hands down the main reason why high performers consistently outperform everyone else. The high performers who make a shit-ton of money and who the bots won't beat are masters of creating personalized value. They are experts at the H2H sale, personalizing the experience a customer has in a way that can't be imitated. It's how they became invaluable to their customers, who simply don't want to buy from anyone else...ever.

Personalized value is how a salesperson like Bill took his relationship with Alpha Corp to a far more meaningful and lucrative level than his predecessor Jennifer did. Although Jennifer was delivering on general and company value, she didn't understand personalized value.

Bill was able to create personalized value because he took the time to do thoughtful discovery and learn more about the customer. He found ways he could help the IT director look good to the new CIO. He then went on to create personalized value for the CIO by helping him get a firm grip on the current state of IT in Alpha Corp's business, something that might have taken the CIO months or even years to learn on his own. He did this knowing that the CIO was under a lot of pressure to establish himself at the company that had recruited him expecting certain results. He helped the CIO's team understand what innovation meant at Alpha Corp and how to deliver on the CIO's desire for more innovation. Bill was a master of H2H and personalized value. I think you can be, too.

CREATING VALUE

As a salesperson, your goal is to drive value, rather than just volume. This may be counterintuitive, particularly if you sell in a primarily transactional environment. You're expected to sell as much as you can; volume is critical. To win at the H2H level for the long term, however, you have to focus on creating value. It's not the *volume* of what you sell, but the *value* of what you sell and how you sell. It's not good enough to be a *conveyor* of value: you have to be a *purveyor* of value. You must learn what value really means to the customer and then do whatever it takes to realize that value for them. Sometimes, what is valuable to a customer has little or nothing to do, at least directly, with the actual product or solution you're selling. It may be your customer just wants to look good to their boss and climb the corporate ladder. It's on you to be able to show how what you are selling is going to help them do that. You determine how to make your solution help customers achieve their goals; you are the purveyor of value.

YOUR KEY TAKEAWAY

Any dummy can stutter and stumble through general and company value points. That's what everyone is expected to do. High performing sales professionals, though, are masters at personalizing value. Personalized value is the only thing that truly differentiates. It's unique, often unexpected, and can never be replicated. It's what endears you to your customer and makes you irreplaceable. You have to become a purveyor of personalized value. You gotta get good at uncovering, creating, and delivering personalized value. You can't beat the bots without it.

CHAPTER 3

MIND THE MIND

The mind is like an iceberg. It floats with
one-seventh of its bulk above water.

—Sigmund Freud

Psychology is at the heart of sales. Don't let anyone tell you otherwise. If you can perceive the rational and emotional forces at work in your customer's mind, you can develop a message that is relevant and persuasive. The more psychological principles you learn, the more effective you will be at creating personalized, differentiated value.

It's crucial to ask high-yield or open-ended questions to understand your customers, ascertain what is valuable to them, and create personalized value. However, you can't just go in and start asking probing questions straight away. That'd be creepy, and creepy is never an option. You have to earn the right to ask those deeper questions. You do that by building rapport and developing your customer's trust.

Here's where psychology is the golden ticket; you can use persuasion and basic psychology to effectively build trust and rapport with your customer pretty quickly. In this chapter, I'm going to teach you a few of these psychological principles and persuasion techniques so that you can earn the right to ask your customers the important questions faster. These are simple and easy and can make an enormous difference in helping you reach your goals as a salesperson.

I know some salespeople aren't interested in psychology and will be tempted to skip ahead to the next chapter. That's cool. Just don't say I didn't warn you. And don't be surprised when you lose a deal to someone who does use psychology and persuasion techniques to win.

The psychological principles outlined in this chapter are used to varying degrees by all top sales performers. Many high-performing sales professionals leverage these techniques instinctively, but you may need to practice them before they become intuitive.

THE RIDER, ELEPHANT, AND PATH

The best way to understand how to drive behavior change is to imagine a rider sitting on an elephant at the beginning of a path. New York University social psychologist Jonathan Haidt explains that in this metaphor, the rider represents the rational system of the brain and the elephant represents the emotional system. The path represents the steps the emotional and rational parts of the brain need to take to reach their destination.

The metaphor tells us that the rational rider relies on evidence, data, and analysis to pick a direction. But the rider can't go anywhere alone—the elephant has to power the journey.

The emotional elephant's behavior is influenced by its experiences and feelings. The elephant is horribly afraid of risk, loss, and pain. He hates change; he likes the comfort of sameness.

The rider and elephant look at things differently, and this poses potential conflicts between the rational and emotional systems of the brain.

Who do you think will win? Who do you think will determine to change or not to change, to move or not to move—the five-ton elephant or the little dude sitting on top? The elephant, of course. The rider can tell the elephant where to go or what to do over and over again. He can cajole, nudge, push, or pull him, but the elephant is emotional, not rational, and isn't going to budge if he doesn't feel like it. He can crush the rider if he wants to.

This metaphor is particularly relevant in our world. In B2B sales, you're asking customers to change behavior and make a big decision. All B2B sales involve change, but technology sales often require customers to make significant changes on many levels. If we want our customers to change their behavior or make a decision in our favor, we must address both the rational and emotional systems of their minds. The rider needs enough data to analyze, and the elephant needs the courage to change and move.

The rider and elephant also must understand the path and how they are going to navigate it. If they feel the path is full of obstacles, poses any threats, or is just plain risky, they won't move. Both must believe the path is safe and makes sense.

In practical terms for a B2B tech sales professional, the path is the process our customer goes through to achieve the results we promised. This may include the sales process, implementation, and the steps they must take to recognize the value they signed for.

You must reckon with all three aspects of the metaphor: the rider, the elephant and the path. First, you must direct the rider (your customer's rational mind). Second, you have to motivate the elephant (your customer's emotional mind). Throughout, you have to help shape the path for the rider and elephant and show them that you have addressed risk as well as rational and emotional obstacles they perceive ahead. Here's how:

- **Direct the Rider:** We know the rider is logical, analytical, and data-oriented, so we must provide our buyers with enough objective facts, data, and evidence to enable them to decide in our favor. This data includes such things as technical features and corresponding benefits, various metrics, service level agreements (SLAS), customer success survey information, and any other information that would persuade them to buy from you. Give them the information they need to make the decision—no more, no less. Riders love data and analysis so much that they can become overwhelmed and unable to do anything if they are given too much.

They go into "analysis paralysis" mode, and your deal will get stuck.

- **Motivate the Elephant:** Inspiring that big emotional elephant to change its current behavior is often the hardest part of your sales cycle. Get comfortable navigating that world of feelings and other mushy stuff. The elephant has deep fears and despises risk. He represents the primal instinct to survive, and it's never easy to mess with primal instincts. However, some things work like elephant fuel. Look for opportunities to create hope for a better future, a sense of safety, or a sense of eliminating risk or avoiding loss. Learn what your customers need to believe and what they need to trust in order to make the purchase—and then make those things happen. Making them believe is not always easy, especially for old elephants who use thirty-year-old technology and fear they'll lose their job if they take risks. Those elephants are much harder to motivate. Focus on creating confidence that whatever you are selling is not going to derail their plans or agenda. Have them talk to other customers who have seen great success with purchases they have made from you. Introduce your customer to the team of individuals who will care for them after the deal is done, making sure those people are likable and can show how much they care. Explain how your customers can win if they decide to buy from you. To become a high-performing sales professional who can beat the bots, you have to show customers that you have their best interests at heart and create psychological safety for them. If you don't get good at elephant whispering, your deals will require more time and effort, and you will not win as much. Figure out what the elephant fuel is for your customer, then fill 'er up.

- **Shape the Path:** Your customer's purchase puts them on a journey to change. The path represents what they have to do to change their behavior and see positive results. You must make it a path of least resistance. How will they make what they purchased realize the intended value? What is needed to ensure adoption? What is the path to achieving ROI? Make it clear to your customers how they will move forward with your solution and what benefits they will see. Tell them about any potential challenges and show them how you will help them remove those obstacles as they implement your solution. If they're moving to a SaaS model for a critical business function, for example, tell them how your service team will help them develop a communication strategy to highlight the benefits to their end users. Explain that you will facilitate adoption using multiple job aids and a formal training webinar for the end users. Help them get comfortable with the journey ahead by preparing them for any challenges and showing them how you will reduce risk and ease their journey. Begin shaping the path early and reinforce that message often throughout your sales cycle.

This powerful metaphor has become the cornerstone of my B2B sales training classes because I've seen it work beautifully for so many sales reps who have adopted it over the years. Sales reps that want to become high performers must get in the habit of asking themselves: Did I direct the rider? Did I motivate the elephant? Did I shape the path? If your deal is stalled, my money says you haven't done these things to the satisfaction and comfort level your customer requires.

This is the new ABC. Forget "Always Be Closing." Today you have to think, "Always Be Considering" the rider, elephant, and path, or "ABC the REP." ABC the REP and you will see immediate, positive results in your customer relationships, more efficiency in your sales cycle, and better deal outcomes. Use this concept of ABC the REP to your advantage; it's the closest thing to a "secret sauce" you are going to find.

ELEPHANT FUEL:
PRINCIPLES OF INFLUENCE

Motivating the elephant is usually the hardest and most complex part of this process to master. To help out with this, I am going to tell you about the teachings of Robert Cialdini on the art of persuasion. Robert Cialdini is a professor emeritus of psychology and marketing at Arizona State University and was a visiting professor of marketing, business, and psychology at Stanford University. He is best known for his research on the principles of persuasion, and his work continues to be a vitally important and influential work on the subject.

Cialdini identified a series of persuasion principles that govern human behavior. His book, *Influence: The Psychology of Persuasion*, explores universal principles that apply to countless situations. I find that these principles are particularly compelling in the world of sales. Let's look at some of Cialdini's persuasion principles that are relevant in sales and how you can apply them as a psychology-savvy sales professional.

Quick disclaimer: these psychological principles of persuasion don't work on all humans. They won't work on sociopaths and, for some reason, my husband. (Just kidding on the husband part. Sort of.)

But since these principles work on most people, learn them and apply them where they make sense throughout your sales motion. If they aren't making a difference, and your customer is not responding at all to any of the following techniques, take a step back and ask yourself if you stand a chance of selling to that individual at all.

RECIPROCITY

This principle tells us that if someone does something for you or gives you something, you will feel an obligation to do something for them in return. The adage "you scratch my back, I'll scratch yours" comes to mind. As soon as somebody does you a favor, you get the urge to repay them, right? (Don't tell me if you don't. Remember my disclaimer about sociopaths? Hmmmm?) This is our nature; it's how our brains are hardwired. The key to using this principle of persuasion in sales is that you should be the first one to give, and what you give should be personalized and unexpected.

Also, if you can do something for your customer—something personalized and unexpected that was done specially for them—then they will be more likely to do something for you, especially if you ask.

There's a biological explanation for this too, as shared by

scientist Paul Zak.[3] When someone gives or receives a gift, a hormone called oxytocin is released. It's linked to trust and connectedness, which we know are foundational in complex selling. That oxytocin hit can make the customer more willing to trust, increase the connection with the giver, and make the receiver want to reciprocate.

Years ago, I was working with a sales professional named Corey, who told me about Mark, an IT director that needed to invest in cloud technology per the CIO's direction. Mark didn't know where to start or how to get buy-in from the higher-ups, including his CIO.

Corey struggled to reach the next level in his relationship with Mark. He hadn't even been able to get Mark to have lunch with him; it was always just teleconference or meeting in Mark's office. I explained reciprocity to Corey and asked him if there was anything he could do for the IT director or give to the IT director that would be beneficial for him or help him in some way. After some brainstorming, Corey had a great idea.

---

3   Paul J. Zak, Robert Kurzban, William T. Matzner. "Oxytocin is associated with human trustworthiness." *Hormones and Behavior.* 2005. https://www.semanticscholar.org/paper/Oxytocin-is-associated-with-human-trustworthiness-Zak-Kurzban/cde617cc3f07faa62ed3812ee150c20559bb91cd

Corey researched ways to get internal buy-in when making significant IT investments. He found a couple of excellent articles in reputable publications. He highlighted relevant sections and included notes that tied back to comments and information Mark had shared with him. Corey emailed the files to the IT director with a quick note: "Hi Mark, I know you're trying to figure out the best way to get the execs on board with your cloud strategy. I did some research for you, and I came across the attached articles I thought you might find helpful. I highlighted the points that I think you'll find most relevant. Take a look and let me know if you have any questions or would like to discuss this information and my notes over lunch."

BOOM.

Corey showed Mark that he was willing to go out of his way to help him succeed. A few days later, Mark thanked Corey via email and accepted Corey's invitation to lunch.

At lunch, Mark said he was surprised and impressed with Corey's efforts to help him. Corey proposed they put together a presentation and jointly walk through it with the CIO, and Mark enthusiastically agreed.

That's reciprocity. Corey's "gift" of research and information to Mark had triggered a sense of obligation and a need to reciprocate. Mark previously would not agree to lunch, much less a CIO meeting, but after Corey's thoughtful research, Mark agreed to *both*.

Corey continued to apply various tools and techniques throughout the sales cycle and was able to close a multimillion-dollar, five-year contract for cloud and other IT services for that customer. Later, Mark moved on to another company and Corey had no trouble getting a meeting with him there and closing another big deal. Reciprocity is a form of persuasion which, when coupled with sincerity and a genuine desire for a customer to succeed, can accelerate and supersize your deals. Just remember, *personalized* and *unexpected* are the keys to successfully using this principle.

AUTHORITY

People will almost always respond better to a perceived authority figure than to you, my dear sales professionals. In the context of a deal, authority figures can influence and persuade others better than a salesperson. For example, if your customer hasn't been persuaded by your efforts, or if your deal is stalled, bring someone higher up in your company to meet the customer and help deliver your message. This is also called level-selling—bringing in someone from a higher level at your organization to help you sell or unstick a deal. Your vice president of sales may say the same thing about the product that you've been saying all along, but watch in amazement as the customer suddenly thinks it's gospel. This has far less to do with what was said than who said it. The influence of authority is one major reason why analysts such as Gartner, IDC, and Forrester are relied upon so heavily by B2B technology buyers. Sometimes, it's not real until an authority tells you it's real.

Learn to level sell and bring in a leader to speed up or unstick a deal. Use Gartner, IDC, and Forrester studies to persuade your customer. Look at your prospect's LinkedIn profile to learn who they follow and what groups they are a part of. If a sales professional wants to get to me, for example, they should invoke leadership guru Simon Sinek. If you want me to buy a book, tell me that Simon Sinek said it was an excellent read. If you need me to understand something and get on board with it, use words or examples from Simon Sinek. Sinek is an authority I believe and trust, so there's a 99.9 percent chance I'll follow his advice.

SCARCITY

When someone perceives that something is limited, they are much more likely to want it. The perceived value increases.

Limited-edition anything is an example of this principle at play. Also, when you are shopping for an airline ticket or hotel room on one of the major travel websites, a message often pops up saying "only three seats left at this price" or "only two rooms left." That's an example of the website using scarcity to persuade someone to buy. When I see there is only one airline ticket left at a certain price, I will probably buy it right away rather than procrastinate.

Let's look at an example in our B2B sales world. Say your customer brings up a major IT security-related challenge they are facing. You realize it would be wise to get the security sales engineer in front of this customer, but engineers in B2B tech sales companies are often spread thin.

Instead of saying "I'll set up a meeting with our security engineer who can address your questions," phrase it something like this:

"We have an amazing security engineer. He has incredible experience with what you are talking about and has helped several customers. I know he'll be able to help you. The only problem is that his schedule is packed. Sometimes I have to wait a while to get him on the calendar. But, let me see what I can do."

Your customer is likely going to be eager to make this meeting happen and they may even say something like "Please, the sooner the better." That is the scarcity principle at play. In a situation where trying to set up a meeting with an engineer doesn't create any sense of urgency in your customer, calling out the resource constraint and scarcity will make them take notice and more likely to agree to schedule that follow-up meeting. When you go back to your customer stating that you are able to get on that engineer's calendar early next week, what do you think your customer will say?

They are likely to say something akin to "yeah, I'll make it work." They don't want to lose that "spot" that you have secured on the supertechie's calendar. The added bonus is that you are highlighting how much you want them to succeed, here, and showing that you are willing to do what it takes to help them address their questions and needs.

This only works when what you are saying is true, however. If you have an engineer sitting on his hands, positioning him as God's gift to technology is *not* going to work. Yet, I've never worked for a company where the rockstar sales engineer is waiting for something to do. These resources are scarce, so you are not dishonest or insincere.

Customers have a spidey sense for sales reps who are shoveling BS. Just don't. Insincerity or dishonesty will kill a deal faster than Leisure Suit Larry can say buh-bye. You'll find plenty of other ways to genuinely use the scarcity principle to help you in your sales motion, so avoid using it if something isn't actually scarce.

If your company hosts a speaker about security services, and you're inviting customers to attend, instead of saying, "Hey, we're hosting this event and I think you should come," say something like, "This event is invite-only. I am personally inviting just a few of my customers. I think you would benefit and I'd love you to come." The chances of this customer attending your event are now higher than if you had just sent an email saying, "Join us." The same anti-Larry rule is applicable here: if you are inviting everyone, it's dishonest and shady to suggest this is a rare opportunity. Don't pull a Larry.

SOCIAL PROOF

Social proof means people making a decision will be guided by the actions of others. People are more likely to trust and follow things that have been endorsed by others whom they trust or believe.

The most prominent example of this is our overwhelmingly review-driven approach to buying. Whether we are buying a book, choosing a restaurant, or planning a vacation, we can read reviews from other people. I sometimes feel like I spend more time on Yelp trying to figure out which restaurant people liked best than I do at the actual meal. My husband is the worst, though. If I drag him to a place he hasn't already looked up on Yelp, he will be on his phone reading reviews when we get to the restaurant. Then he will order based on the reviews from people who are at "duke" status. My husband does this all the time. Are you questioning my life choices? Welcome to the club. Hah...

For sales reps, you can best leverage social proof in the following ways:

1. **Customer References.** There's a reason most buyers ask for references. Hearing about your product or service from an existing customer is far more powerful than anything you or someone in your organization could say. Make sure you have customer references that are honest, trustworthy, and genuine. It doesn't work if they sound scripted.

2. **Peers.** If you are working with a prospect CIO and there is another CIO you've sold to who is pleased with you and your company, put your prospect in contact with the existing, satisfied CIO. This process is similar to customer referral but more deliberate in terms of aligning job function or role.

3. **Experts.** This idea is in line with the authority principle we discussed earlier. If you can show some testimonial or approval from an expert in either the buyer's industry or from your industry, that will help persuade the buyer. Who does your customer consider to be an authority in their space? Is there an industry thought leader out there your buyers follow? Leverage blog posts, content, and quotes from these individuals. Share content with a brief note on why you believe that insight is worth sharing with the client.

Now you have some powerful principles of persuasion to put in your sales motion. Except...nothing is ever *that* straightforward, is it? Nope. Neither are these silver bullets.

Remember Larry? Larry is why words like slimy, sneaky, and shady come up when others talk about salespeople. Larry misused the principles of persuasion and other laws of human nature to take advantage of people. Look where it got him. These principles only work if you use them with integrity and honesty. To be effective, these principles must be used with good intent. People know when they are being manipulated or "sold."

To work in an H2H way that machines can't replicate, you have to lean on the humanness of it all. This includes remembering things like the Golden Rule ("do unto others..."). You must genuinely want to help your customer succeed and to add value to your interactions with them. Sincerity is a prerequisite. Personalizing value and creating long-lasting relationships only happens when there is trust. Trying to manipulate customers with the principles of persuasion will backfire every time. And it's not pretty, trust me, I have seen deals and relationships break because of even the most subtle bit of manipulation. If you can't be honest and don't sincerely want to help the customer succeed, don't bother trying.

Use these concepts to help you do right by the customer and to facilitate their success. These principles will help your buyers make decisions in your favor *only* if combined with sincerity and trust. You have been warned. If you use your newly learned persuasive powers for evil, the karma police are going to find you and your commission check.

YOUR KEY TAKEAWAY

Psychology is foundational to good selling. Learn the basics and use them to help guide your buyers in making good buying decisions. Use the principles of persuasion wisely.

If you cannot find it in your heart to genuinely want to help your customer succeed or win, then don't even try to use them, or any other concept in this book. It won't work. It will probably backfire in an ugly way. Just don't.

CHAPTER 4

DISCOVERY: UNLOCKING KNOWLEDGE

If I had an hour to solve a problem and my life depended on the solution, I would spend the first 55 minutes determining the proper questions to ask.

—Albert Einstein

The process of discovery—asking questions to learn and understand more about your customer—is crucial if you want to be a high-performing sales professional. It's vital that you collect as much information as possible throughout the sales cycle. You can't articulate a meaning-ful value proposition for your customer if you don't know what they need and value. Remember, value is in the eye of the customer.

Here's an example I learned from a mentor early in my career that illustrates how critical effective discovery is for a sales professional.

David was a pharmaceutical sales rep who sold a medica-tion specifically for attention-deficit/hyperactivity disorder (ADHD). David frequently called on a physician, Dr. Charles, who treated patients with ADHD. David catered lunches for the office, had a great relationship with the staff, brought in holiday baskets for everyone, and practiced other "rela-tionship building" activities throughout the year. The staff and Dr. Charles were grateful and always welcomed David warmly. The problem was that David could never get Dr. Charles to write prescriptions for ADHD medication.

At one point, David's regional manager, Michael, was con-cerned about David's inability to actually sell to the phy-sician. Michael decided to do a ride-along with David to Dr. Charles' practice. The office was welcoming, as always, and Dr. Charles was happy to meet with David and Michael. After some small talk, Michael asked Dr. Charles, "So, Dr.

Charles, tell me about how you select which medication to prescribe to your ADHD patients?"

Dr. Charles had surmised that Michael was really asking why the doctor had never prescribed the medication they were selling.

"That's a great question," Dr. Charles replied. "I would love to prescribe your medication, but most of my patients are kids who have disruptive behavioral problems at school. I need a medication that kicks in quickly. Your medication takes six weeks to become effective. I can't give these kids medicine that takes so long to kick in. They would be expelled by then."

You want to facepalm for David, don't you? Imagine how he felt.

David had been calling on Dr. Charles for almost a year and never learned this critical piece of information! Since the ground couldn't open up and swallow David whole, which he probably would have preferred, he had to continue to listen to the conversation between Michael and Dr. Charles.

"Wow, I did not know that!" Michael said. "Thanks for explaining it. I understand your point. But I have to tell you this medication is far superior to the one you currently prescribe. It addresses symptoms much more effectively than other medications."

"Yes, I've heard it's a good drug," the doctor said, glancing at David.

"What if you were to prescribe our medication to the children who you see at the end of the school year or early in the summer?" Michael asked. "That way, the medicine kicks in over the summer and by the time they go back to school, they have experienced the benefits. Wouldn't it be worth giving a subset of your patients this medication so that they could, at least, have the best results?"

Dr. Charles nodded agreeably. "Great idea," he said. "I'd be willing to try it out in that scenario."

I would have *loved* to have been a fly on the (inside, obv.) windshield of the car when Michael and David rode back to the office. I can only imagine what Michael said to David about making such a rookie mistake. *One question* could have changed the entire sales cycle and resulted in a win.

You have to get disciplined about asking questions. I know that is easier said than done. When you're in the middle of a selling situation, especially one where the conversation is flowing well, you might not realize you didn't ask some basic questions. But know that missing the answers to those questions will often delay or kill a deal.

What value looks like to one customer can be very different than the next one. You do yourself and your company a big disservice if you don't make the time to ask questions that help you clearly see what value means to that one human being that you are selling to. Only then can you articulate a value proposition that is meaningful and relevant to them.

RESEARCH INFORMS DISCOVERY

Discovery begins before you meet your customer, through research. Do as much research as you can. Go through the company's website to understand its mission, vision, and history, of course, but also Google the company. Look for news, financial information, reviews, and whatever else looks interesting. Don't forget to look at LinkedIn, Twitter, and any other social media platform where the company has a presence. If someone in your LinkedIn network is a connection of the person you are meeting or anyone else at the prospect, ask that contact if they have information they can share. Your contact might introduce you to their connection, who may have all kinds of inside intel for you.

Research whatever you can while staying on the right side of creepy. That research ensures you ask relevant questions whose answers are not easily found on the website.

By the way, customers are likely doing the same thing with you. They've researched your company. They've been on your LinkedIn profile. Customers value their time and they want to ensure you aren't wasting theirs.

In Leisure Suit Larry's days, sellers had all the information and buyers were relatively clueless and at the mercy of the salesperson. Today, car buyers know every damn thing before they even get to the dealership. They know the car they want and the price of that car at every dealer in the area. They know how online sites have priced the car. Like car buyers, B2B customers are arming themselves with as much information as possible before making a major purchase. The internet has created a B2B sales landscape where buyers have a lot more knowledge and power than they ever have before.

WHAT KIND OF A QUESTION IS THAT?

Our goal as sales professionals is to develop a value proposition that makes what we are selling a no-brainer for the customer to purchase. To do this, you have to dig deep to learn what matters most to that customer. If you don't ask, you won't know how to position your offering in a manner that can differentiate it from the others.

You've all been told to use open-ended questions for discovery. That's good advice, but I want you to call the kinds of questions you need to ask "high impact questions," or HI-QS. Think of these as open-ended questions on steroids. HI-QS are designed to give you the most bang for your buck during discovery. I call them "high-impact questions" because they have high impact answers that help you sharpen your message. They aren't your everyday open-ended questions. Take a look:

Average open-ended question	High impact question (HI-Q)
Who are your direct reports?	Can you help me understand your organizational structure?
How well does IT partner with the business?	How would you describe IT's role within your business?
What are some of your IT initiatives?	Can you explain how your planned IT initiatives support the company's business objectives?
What roles have you held at this company?	Tell me about your career here at X Corp.

Your questions should begin with something like, "help me understand," "how do you feel?" or "what do you think?" Average open-ended questions may get you better than a "yes" or "no" answer, but they aren't going to get you the most important information. Also, when you ask questions using these openers, you are showing the customer you care and that you aren't just interrogating them; you want to understand them, their perspective, and how they feel about it. There's a reason a gazillion shrinks ask questions this way.

This is not as simple as it sounds. In my career, I've seen high-level sales leaders neither understand this nor do it effectively. Top performing sales reps consistently ask high impact questions. For them, it's typically intuitive. Of course, not everyone walks around asking questions a shrink would be jealous of. But you can learn how, practice and go into discovery meetings with a mental list of HI-QS to ask.

Many successful transactional salespeople are taught to ask basic yes or no questions so they can quickly move through a conversation and get to the sale. That approach works in simple, straightforward sales, so these salespeople continue to use it. Before they go into the meeting, they have an idea of what product they want to sell that customer.

They ask closed-ended questions to get the answers they need to get the order so they can move on to the next sale.

When it comes to more complex sales, you must ask more detailed HI-Q questions that tie to the business and help you understand the person you're talking to. You need this information because it is harder to differentiate in complex sales. What's more, you have to continue asking those HI-Q questions throughout your engagement with the customer. You are always doing discovery because you can get information that strengthens your value proposition and increases your chances of winning. You need to ask specific questions that help you with shaping your messaging for the *rider*, *elephant*, and *path* as we discussed in chapter three.

I'll give you some sample questions in the next chapter, but first I'll tell you a story about what can go wrong if you don't ask the right questions—or all of the questions.

I was working on a pursuit team for Omnitech, a large technology solutions provider. We were trying to sell to an existing Omnitech customer who had been with the company for years. The customer company, let's call them Beta Corp, had a new CIO that was brought in to help modernize the organization. He wanted his talented technology employees working on improving the overall business, not managing phone systems and video conferencing. The CIO wanted to outsource those tasks, and boy did we want that business.

Omnitech had won deals for various small projects over the past decade. We introduced ourselves to the CIO and shared with him how we'd gotten along well with his team for many years and how those conversations helped us understand the team's needs. We highlighted our relationship with Beta Corp because we felt that was our competitive differentiator. We also wanted the CIO to know we would make him look good because of all the insight we could share with him about his team and the organization he had just joined. We had plenty of elephant fuel, and we could tell that he regarded us favorably. At one point, he even asked us if we would help pull together a PR campaign to help elevate the IT team in the eyes of the business. This deal looked like it was in the bag.

We lost. The reason? We didn't ask the right questions to help us see the big picture.

We assumed our company had developed a great relationship with Beta Corp over the years. We knew there had been periodic service delivery issues in the past year, but we thought the problems were day-to-day blips that were quickly addressed. That's what we had been led to believe by the internal service delivery organization.

In reality, Beta Corp was utterly dissatisfied with our work and frustrated with our company's extensive service delivery issues.

The CIO was looking for a partner to facilitate a massive change. His elephant didn't just need to know that we had a long-standing relationship with the company or that we understood the business as it had been over the past few years we had worked with Beta Corp. The CIO's elephant also needed to know that our company would not let him fail, that signing with us for this massive change would not be high risk. He needed to know that the path ahead in a partnership with us would not be a rocky one. We had already shown that we were a risky option, given our poor performance, and we didn't shape the path in a way that reassured the CIO. The CIO likely felt that we would let him fail by not delivering services to the level that he required—a level that we hadn't been able to perform at for a long time.

The competition came in with a clean slate, in this regard. They had no noteworthy prior relationship with Beta Corp and cost significantly more, but the elephant felt safer signing on with the new provider. The winning company sold the CIO on the idea that they could remove the risk and that they had a record of exceptional delivery for companies just like Beta Corp. It was not a tough decision for the elephant. The CIO himself didn't have the longstanding relationship with Omnitech or the trust and confidence that came with it. He was new and focused on proving his own value to those who hired him. The elephant merely wanted to feel safe on a path without obstacles. He needed to know that he wouldn't regret his decision on such an important initiative.

We never saw this big picture because we didn't ask the right questions throughout the sales cycle. Imagine how things might have gone if early on the sales team had asked the CIO, "What could prevent you from wanting to go with us?" That question would have given the CIO or his direct reports a chance to explain how dissatisfied they were with our company's service. If we had asked more high-impact questions, they could have indicated they were nervous about putting such a large, high-profile piece of business in the hands of a company that had proven it was good at dropping the ball. If we had learned this, we could have addressed *that* issue instead of focusing on how great our relationship was. We could have asked what we could do to give the CIO the comfort level he needed. If what he needed to feel confident wasn't something we could make into a reality, we may have decided not to invest so much effort into a lost cause.

But we didn't ask those high-impact questions. We made flawed assumptions. We were just like the pharmaceutical rep selling ADHD medication who had gotten so focused on rapport and relationship that he never questioned why the physician wasn't writing prescriptions for the medication he represented.

Deliberately use high-impact questions to learn every nook of the sales context and shape your messaging. ABC the REP. If you don't address the rational and the emotional needs of your customer—the rider *and* the elephant—it won't matter how well-positioned you seem to be. If you don't show them that the path will not be risky, they won't go with you. Ask the questions that will help you to address the REP. The next chapter we'll work on how to do this.

YOUR KEY TAKEAWAY

Your average old open-ended questions aren't enough to get you the information you need to truly differentiate from your competition and the bots. Get comfortable using high-impact questions that you'll think make you sound like a shrink. There's a reason people tell therapists everything. Open your questions with "help me under-stand," "can you explain," and "how would you describe." Questions like this force the customer to give you not just a little more than a yes or no but a hell of a lot more. It's the only way you will be able to message and persuade the rider and elephant to want to move and figure out how to shape the path so that they'll actually do it.

CHAPTER 5

ABC THE REP

The mind can be convinced, but the heart must be won.

—Simon Sinek

Getting phone calls from my previous clients who have been successful with ABC the REP is one of my favorite things in the world. My son even uses this strategy to navigate the insanity of junior high. (I can't lie; I love those stories too.)

ALWAYS BE CONSIDERING THE RIDER, ELEPHANT, PATH

As you probably remember from chapter 3, Haidt's rider, elephant, and path metaphor can help appeal to the mind of a Fortune 500 CIO or of the eighth-grade math teacher you are trying to convince not to give you a zero for a missed assignment. To change behavior, you want to Always Be Considering the Rider, Elephant, (and) Path. ABC the REP.

Focused, high-impact questions can help you determine what matters to the rider and the elephant and will show you how to navigate the path ahead. With this information, you will understand what is valuable to your customers and how to deliver both what they want *and* what they need. In this chapter, I will show you sample questions to ask your customer in order to Direct the Rider, Motivate the Elephant, and Shape the Path. Because it's more difficult to reach the emotional elephant than the rational rider, I've included additional questions to help you motivate the elephant.

DIRECT THE RIDER

The rational rider likes data, objective information, and strong evidence. He may get overwhelmed when presented with too many options, though, so limit his choices. Don't try to reinvent the wheel in your communications with the rider. Figure out what works and follow that model. Ultimately, you have to make sure the rider sees a clear, direct path forward.

The following simple, straightforward questions are ideal for the early stage of relationship building with your customer. These examples, like most in this book, address a B2B technology buyer, but the principle of directing the rider is applicable in any sale. Feel free to tailor these questions for relevancy, depending on the level and personnel you are selling to within an organization.

RIDER-ORIENTED QUESTIONS

What are your service-level agreements
(SLAS) and other key metrics?

What is working well, today? Why?

What are your key initiatives for this year?
What projects are you working on?

How do you allocate the budget for your IT investments?

How do you determine which business initiatives to support?

What types of information can we provide
to help you make your decision?

Most of these questions will elicit basic answers that keep you centered on the logical, rational, and objective realm of the sale. You may get a response like, "Let me pull out a list of all the projects that we're working on," and the customer may even walk through their spreadsheet with you. That's the rider opening up. You need the information the customer shares with you about his projects because this information represents what is important to him. The rider is likely showing you that completing these projects is valuable for this particular buyer. This gives you insight as to how you can personalize your messaging to target exactly what matters to him. In this simple exchange, you have learned that you can come back with a proposal that indicates how your product or service will help the buyer execute on these projects more quickly and efficiently. The more specific you can be in referencing what you have learned about the projects from the rider here, the better.

Sometimes, you may ask a rider-oriented question, intending to get a logical, data-based answer, yet powerful emotions will lead to an elephant answer. This tells you a lot about the customer and their mindset; that five-ton elephant is definitely in charge. Another customer, faced with the same question about prioritizing projects, may respond with something like, "I can show you the list of projects but it's not like I have a choice in any of it. We do whatever the CEO yells about most at any given point." This answer shows you the same list of projects you can use to address the rider in your proposal, just as in the previous example; however, the customer has *also* just carried you straight into elephant territory. Let me just tell you—you *love* visiting elephant territory.

This is where you find meaningful details to create the personalized value that will move the customer to buy.

Think through the customer's answer for a minute. What is she telling you? She feels that her opinion is not taken seriously or that she can't influence the prioritization of her own department's projects. Perhaps, for some reason, the buyer is not considered credible and trustworthy by the leadership team. You have an opening to deliver personalized value to this customer by finding ways to help her elevate herself within her organization. Once she has shown the elephant a little, you have an opportunity to begin asking more elephant-oriented questions. As you do, she will likely share more about her frustrations. When you message this customer during proposal or presentation, you can direct the rider with messages targeting project completion. You can also motivate the elephant by indicating how your organization will help highlight her team's value to the leadership, giving them a better chance of influencing decisions such as what projects they work on.

Remember that CIO from the previous chapter, the one whose business had been unsatisfied with our company's levels of service? If we had asked him what information he needed from us, he could have answered that he required a list of certifications or customer references. Those are things that appeal to the rational rider. On the other hand, he may have said, "Well, you might want to start with consistently meeting your SLAs." This is a much more meaningful answer because it shows emotion: the elephant did not feel safe. People who don't feel safe won't buy from you. Why would they take such a risk?

MOTIVATE THE ELEPHANT

Elephant questions, as we have already touched on, are questions used to bring out a person's emotional needs and desires. Questions that engage the elephant will help you determine how to motivate it to make the change you are selling. Just as you must direct the rider in order to get a buyer ready to move, you have to motivate the elephant to actually go.

The elephant has to be drawn out, because most people won't readily reveal their emotions in a professional setting. It's important to remember that the elephant isn't going to come out unless it feels safe. If you walk into an initial customer meeting and immediately start asking about career goals or other elephant-style questions, the customer is going to think you're creepy, which will keep you from ever getting invited back. You have to *earn* the right to engage the elephant. If you haven't built rapport or developed trust, your customer is not going to offer up emotional responses. Also, remember to be authentic. If you aren't comfortable showing emotion or vulnerability, the customer most certainly won't be.

Trust is the ticket that gets you access to elephant territory. You can't create personalized value unless you have spent some time poking around in elephant territory. So, let's look at the types of questions that will earn you that ticket.

ELEPHANT-ORIENTED QUESTIONS

Imagine it's a year from now, and you're looking back over the past year. What would make you say, "I was a huge success last year"?

This question is designed to help you understand your customer's motivators. One client may say, for example, "My team will be focused on business-differentiating activities, not just tactical technical support." An answer like this tells you that the client takes her role as a leader seriously. She cares about her team's success and equates it with her own success. You do not want to let her feel as if what you are selling will minimize her team's efforts or, heaven forbid, put them out of a job. Lord help you if suggest that she should "outsource" any functions her team owns. As you learn more, you will likely determine that one key to motivating this elephant is messaging that highlights the value of her team's time and talent.

On the other hand, a customer who says "I will have been promoted to VP" is clearly more self-oriented. It is likely that he is ambitious and equates the idea of success with a promotion and higher-level title. You can use this knowledge to guide additional questions for insight into what is required for him to achieve that promotion. Once you know this, you will be able to position your offering in the context of helping him achieve the objectives that will take him to the next level. In this case, one key to motivating this elephant is elevating his ego by showing why your solution will accelerate his rise to a VP role, and how it will do so.

How does the business perceive the role of IT?

In the hundreds of times I have earned the right and asked this question, I've never had the answer come without palpable emotion—ever. If the business perceives that the IT team generates value, they likely have some power and influence within the company. Business-savvy IT professionals are motivated by opportunities to leverage technology to gain a business advantage. If you are selling to a team that's intertwined with the business, you will need to articulate your solution's value in business terms and show how your solution drives the desired outcomes.

If the customer indicates that the business perceives IT as being a service delivery organization or a utility provider, that's very different. This tells you there is room for IT to elevate within the organization. These customers may say something like, "IT doesn't have a seat at the table." In this case, you should emphasize your solution's value around helping IT improve the perception of their contribution to the company. Of course, you will ask a lot more questions to get a deeper understanding of what this means so you can tailor your messaging. The elephant in this situation wants a seat at the table; it's on you to show how your products and services will create the business value and recognition to make this happen.

Finally, you may hear a response such as, "They think that we blow them off and aren't responsive," or "They're always complaining about how long it takes us to resolve their tickets." This is what I like to call the Land Cruiser Express to elephant territory. These answers tell you that IT is perceived negatively, maybe even as failing. Ask more questions to figure out why they can't resolve tickets and why they aren't seen as responsive to the business. Show them how your product addresses the obstacles that make them seem slow or unresponsive. This will get you the fuel with which to motivate the elephant.

How do you address pressure to "innovate" from your leadership team?

Some customers will tell you, "There is no pressure." The elephant isn't ready; move on.

An IT buyer who does have a seat at the table may say something like, "The business is looking for us to provide recommendations around innovation." That's more of a rider answer, devoid of emotion, but now you've learned there is an expectation for the IT team to address innovation.

Or, you may get an answer similar to this: "Our CEO talks about innovation, but he doesn't even really know what it is; he just heard this buzzword in his peer group, and then he comes in and tells us to innovate. Like we don't have enough to worry about around here." Ding ding ding! This is an emotional response that tells you a lot about the buyer's relationship with the CEO, how he is perceived within the organization, and how much pressure he is under.

Through asking several more questions, you will be able to help the customer identify and articulate what innovation means in their world. Then, you show him how your solution will help them innovate as well as alleviate the overwhelming pressure he is feeling. If you really want some elephant fuel, show him how to message this to the executive team so that he can cement his position as an innovative IT leader.

Where do you see your career going at this company?

If the customer answers, "You know what? There's no career path here," you can surmise that he is complacent and isn't really fired up about showing his value to the business. It also may be an indicator that you will need to focus closely on creating urgency around the need to change. Proceed by asking questions to ascertain what he believes his career should look like, whether he is at the current company or another one. Your messaging, then, will highlight how to help him get to the next level in his career. Show that implementing your solution will gain him the credibility and experience he needs to fast track his career goals.

If, on the other hand, he says, "I want to be a COO," then find out how you can help him get there. It doesn't have to be anything monumental; it could be as simple as calling out some IT-related operational issues he mentioned and carefully detailing how your solution will address them and increase efficiency. Portray your information with links back to operational efficiency, increased productivity, and the resulting cost reductions. The elephant fuel, here, is in messaging that aligns with his personal career objective of becoming a COO.

How can you make your team more successful?

The answer to this question will show you how much the customer cares about the success of his existing team. Because your technology solution could result in cuts to the staff, gaining this insight is crucial. Is this customer someone who is so terrified about losing his staff that you can't say anything to indicate that his team would in any way be negatively impacted by doing business with your company? You may have a panicky elephant on your hands here. Your goal is to indicate the solution will help make that team more successful and show how it will do so. You must eliminate any perceived risk to the existing IT team, which the leader is very protective of.

Maybe, though, your customer is eager to reassign long-timers who don't believe in cutting-edge technology. Let me give you an example on how to motivate the elephant, here.

I once sold to a small company with a three-person IT team and a new CIO. Donovan, the leader of that IT team, had been there for years, and he had inflated his own value within the company so much that he had the entire organization convinced it would crumble if anything happened to him. Donovan did anything he wanted and easily received funding for his oddball technology schemes. He was practically holding the new CIO hostage.

The CIO told me that he had to "help make sure the company understands that our success and failure does not rest on Donovan's shoulders." In this case, making the team more successful meant either to lose Donovan or convince him that he was not God's gift to the company. So, we were able to indicate that our services automated manual processes that Donovan typically handled. We had to show that implementing our solution meant the company would not be brought to its knees without Donovan.

I also tactfully helped Donovan recognize that the company's reliance on him was not good for his career. How could he move forward if they didn't think they could survive without him in his current role? This struck a chord with Donovan, who then, wanted to execute on the new CIO's vision more and opened his eyes to job opportunities outside the company. The elephant fuel was overflowing as I told the CIO that I had been coaching Donovan in this manner.

As you ask this question, your answer will tell you whether the team in place is successful or if there is room for improvement. You have to be clear on this answer because your elephant-motivating messages will be very different depending on which direction the response goes.

What does your leadership expect from you?

This question is interesting because it could easily lead to either a rider answer or an elephant answer. The rider response involves a customer essentially going through the bullets on her performance management paperwork. She'll share what she is measured on or what objectives she needs to achieve. The elephant response, however, is more subjective and will show the emotion associated with how the customer perceives they are performing. For example, she may indicate that leadership needs her to become more proactive. You will want to understand what she is doing that would make the leader think she is being reactive. Understanding both her emotions and the criteria for how to live up to her boss's expectations will help you to position your solution. To motivate the elephant in this case, the solution must clearly establish that it will enable the customer to be perceived as proactive and how it will do that.

SHAPE THE PATH

Finally, let's look at questions that will help you determine how to shape the path forward for the customer. The path represents the external environment, but I've found it helpful to think of the path as the steps a buyer has to take in order to achieve his stated goal through the use of any given technology. In other words, now that you have convinced the buyer to move by appealing to both their rational and emotional systems, you have to give them direction and show them that the path is not riddled with obstacles.

As you go through your rider and elephant questions, you will inevitably learn where your customer thinks they need to end up with technology you are positioning. You have to ensure that their view is accurate—and provide clarity if it isn't. Then, you must show them that you will actually help shape the path for them. The customer needs to see how using your offering puts him on the path of least resistance. Give him the comfort that, in partnering with you and your company, there is minimal risk along the path because you will remove obstacles as he goes forward.

Going down the path must seem easy if you want them even to take a first step.

The path questions aim to understand what the customer is afraid of in terms of the consequences associated with the purchase. What are their concerns about adoption or implementation, for example? Once a deal is made, what are they worried will be the roadblocks to realizing the return on their investment?

You already likely understand the reality of what the path of implementation and adoption entails because of your past experiences with customers. So, shaping the path is probably the easiest part of this whole equation. You just have to be able to address the path-related fears of both the rider and the elephant and then show how you will address those fears on the journey. Let's take a look at some questions that will help you achieve your goal of shaping the path.

PATH-ORIENTED QUESTIONS

What risks do you anticipate with this change in technology?

As I mentioned, you have to know what the customer perceives as risky in terms of going forward. Some typical answers to this question that I have heard over the years are:

- Users will not readily adopt the change.
- The business will feel like we are forcing the change upon them.
- We won't achieve our anticipated return if it takes too long to get up and running.

Once you know what the perceived risks are, you set about shaping the path so that the customer's stated risks are minimized or mitigated. Show them that you will provide training content and job aids to help their users adopt more readily. Offer to do a kickoff call with key business stakeholders in order to explain the change and show the company the value that comes from it.

What impact do you think an implementation effort would have on your end users?

This question is similar to the previous one, but we are after something different in asking it. It's very important that when IT organizations make choices, they think through what the business impact is going to be. The implementation of some technology solutions may involve system outages or windows of downtime. Typically, end users can't work during those windows. Although the outages can't be avoided, the frustration that end users experience can be minimized with proactive communication with the business. You can determine, for example, during what timeframe the system is least used and schedule the implementation outage to take place during that window. Then, by communicating what is going to happen with the end users, you minimize the grief your customers would have gotten from the business users during implementation.

What communication strategy will you use to inform your end-user community about an upcoming change such as implementing this solution?

Again, proactive communication can often help minimize frustration. If the customer has a plan in place for communicating changes, you can share some examples of effective communication approaches from other, similar clients. Perhaps you have access to best practice communication programs that you can share with the customer to enhance what they already have in place.

If the customer answers that they do not have any communication strategy in place, this gives you an opportunity to help by providing them with example communications, recommendations around the frequency of communications, or even a list of FAQs that you have compiled based on experience with other clients. (If you don't have this stuff developed, you should. This is one of those precious few differentiators that can be done at a company level. Nudge marketing to help you.) The idea is to show the customer that you have gone down this path before and have in your bag of tricks a variety of ideas and activities that can be used to ease their journey. You want them to know that you have the experience and expertise needed to shape the path for them and can proactively eliminate risk and remove obstacles by providing guidance and direction.

YOUR KEY TAKEAWAY

To help your buyers make buying decisions in your favor, you must appeal to both their hearts and minds. The combination of subjective and objective priorities, combined with any number of different perspectives, makes it tricky to untangle what matters most and why. "Always Be Considering the Rider, Elephant, and Path" means asking questions and using what you learn to create personalized value. The more you consider the REP in your interactions and sales motion, the greater your chance of winning big and building the kind of trust and loyalty that create customers for life.

CHAPTER 6

THE LANGUAGE OF ELEPHANTS

*When dealing with people, remember you are not
dealing with creatures of logic, but creatures of emotion.*
—Dale Carnegie

I f you've done a thorough discovery by asking questions to help you understand rider, elephant, and path, you are ready to take what you've learned and turn it into value.

At the beginning of this book I described three types of value:

1.   **General value:** the inherent value of the product, technology, or solution you are selling.

2.   **Company value:** the value your company creates for the customer, which builds upon the general value.

3.   **Personalized value:** the value created in the H2H relationship, which is as unique as each seller and buyer.

I am trying to drill the idea of personalized value into your mind because creating and delivering it is the only true form of differentiation.

There is no doubt in my mind that you understand the general value of what you are selling. That's table stakes. It comes from even the most basic understanding of the function of the technology you are selling. You can assume that if a customer wants to talk to you, they are at least interested in the general value of the product or solution. You can solidify the general value message for the customer by finding the most effective ways the technology can benefit them, in their world. I am confident that if you are a rep who cares enough about your craft to read this book, you have no issue understanding and articulating the general value of the technology you are selling.

You've also likely spent a significant amount of time learning your company value. This is what your company does differently than other companies selling similar technologies. Think unique value proposition (UVP) or anything remarkable or exceptional that your organization does for the customers. Your company has probably forced you to be at least proficient at communicating the UVP to your customers. What really activates the company value in the eyes of the customer is your ability to show how that value benefits them. You would be amazed at how many sales professionals simply forget to show the benefits of their UVP to the customers themselves. I get it, it can be tough to remember when you're in the middle of the sales cycle. It's just easier to rattle off the value proposition in a pitch or presentation. But your discovery should have given you plenty of details to help make the UVP relevant. Be conscious of this; not tailoring the message to your customer's context is a huge missed opportunity. You don't want to end up sounding like everyone else they talk to.

Personalized value is a crucial concept for you to understand. This is what happens when you take who you are, what you stand for, and what you know and bring it all together to create ways to help your customer win in their own world.

LEARN TO SPEAK ELEPHANTESE

Let's look at a specific example of a time when everything came together to create personal value for a client.

I once worked with a client, Techtronics, that had always been perceived as a company that fulfilled technology orders. The client wanted to be seen as more of a strategic partner. Though customers appreciated the "value-add" Techtronics brought, there was nothing to really differentiate and protect them from losing business to other providers. In one particular sales situation, I was leading the pursuit effort with a Techtronics sales rep on a deal with a team of IT professionals at a prospect account. The customer IT team had admittedly struggled with the business' perception of their contribution to the company. It was important that they create and demonstrate business value in their role, and though they yearned for the "seat at the table" with business leadership, they just couldn't find a way to get there.

I worked with the Techtronics sales rep and team to conduct a discovery session with rider, elephant, and path questions aplenty so we could figure out how to optimize the customer's current IT infrastructure in support of their business objectives. The customer wanted to have outside guidance and a formalized set of recommendations to present to the business in order to help build their credibility.

The Techtronics team went to the customer site to present our findings and recommendations. As we were setting up, I asked Manny, the IT director, if the company had hired the new CIO they had been searching for when we first began working together. Manny nodded and said, "Yes, she started two weeks ago." Typical rider answer for the closed-ended question I had asked. Then Varun, the lead systems engineer who had been with the organization for over a decade, chimed in. "Yeah, and who knows how long we'll all be here, because she is *obsessed* with outsourcing."

Bingo, Elephantese: the most powerful language with which to speak with customers. Varun was afraid of the team losing their jobs under this new, as-yet-unknown CIO. Once that answer came out, Manny joined Varun in elephant territory. "We're very nervous," he said, "because she said some things about how the business is uncertain about what our team actually does and what value we bring."

We already knew from our discovery that the IT team needed to do some PR work to elevate themselves in the eyes of the business. Among other things, I suggested they create a business liaison position and a quarterly newsletter, emphasizing the need to amp up communication between business and IT in order to help create more trust and set them up to be seen as business enablers. I had also recommended a formal communication plan to highlight IT's efforts at ensuring the business was kept apprised of their contributions. They all nodded in agreement, commenting how glad they were for these recommendations because communication was not their forte. Gotta love 'em for being so self-aware and showing vulnerability. It just made me want to help them more.

They mentioned that their new CIO had a background in project management. My experience led me to believe a former project manager would absolutely value a formal communication strategy. As the team walked through the presentation with the customers (and the discussion in the room got more technical than I could stomach), I opened my laptop and began developing a tailored communication plan for them. They noticed I wasn't participating in the conversation, and one of the engineers razzed me a bit. "Hey, we need to get some love from Anita. She's been awfully quiet over there."

I laughed a little and turned my laptop around to show them a spreadsheet with a detailed communication plan.

It was truly customized, even written in their vernacular. I said, "If this isn't love, I don't know what is."

Their response was tremendous: laughter, smiles, thanks all around. They thanked us for helping them think strategically about how to make a good impression with the new CIO. As we were getting ready to leave, Manny said, "I really love the dynamic we all have as a team. It's fun working with you guys. We appreciate how hard you've worked to help make sure we are successful."

I'd put those words pretty high on the list of things that, to a sales professional, sound like a symphony with angels singing. We knew we had really made an impact on them, and we felt confident that they weren't going to want to buy from anybody else. Even though our company didn't have an offering to create communication plans for the customer, it ended up being the most valuable thing for them. How's that for elevating beyond order fulfillment into the realm of strategic partnership? The technical content presented was excellent, don't get me wrong, but it wasn't anything so unique that other companies couldn't create it in some form. It was expected. But when you go above and beyond to proactively address fears, learn to speak in elephant language, and create something uniquely valuable to a customer, it makes all the difference in the world.

Personalized value is the language of elephants. It is based upon a human-to-human interaction, which all begins with establishing trust. Manny and his team had to trust us enough to confide that they felt their jobs were at risk. They had to trust us to know that we had their backs and in no way were we going to try to position our services to somehow replace theirs.

This kind of personalized value can't come from a robot. Only a human can create this depth of trust. Only a human could have determined how badly that IT team needed a communication plan and created it for them, on the spot, in a way that would address the elephant. In this situation, it was my past experience that I was able to leverage to help us differentiate. In other scenarios, it has been another team member's unique expertise or knowledge that helped shape the personalized value we delivered to differentiate. Personalized value is a function of who the seller is, what they know, what they stand for, and how they turn that into something that matters to the customer.

By being elephant whisperers, we made ourselves much more relevant than any competitor or technology website—even one offering better prices. Every other option to buy became invisible to the customers the moment they heard us speak their language: Elephantese, a language of vulnerability, safety, mutual understanding, trust, and partnership. The most memorable and impactful buying experiences are based on how much a customer *feels* you understand them—and how well they feel they understand you.

IT'S PERSONAL FOR YOU, TOO

Part of this understanding means being authentic: comfortable with the things that make you human. Humans are fallible and vulnerable. They're occasionally late. They have children who drive them crazy. They struggle with getting PowerPoint presentations to work. If you embrace this vulnerability and allow glimpses of it to show, you will help your customer trust you more. They will know that you are not perfect—but you are genuine.

Occasionally, I get to work with a, let's say, "self-oriented" sales professional. If I'm scheduled to do a ride-along with this sales person to meet a customer who is also self-oriented, I know I have my work cut out for me. Most of the time, I know within thirty seconds of sitting down at the conference table if the meeting is going to tank. When two egocentric individuals aren't able to get out of their own heads long enough to understand each other, there's little chance of developing the high trust needed to get to elephant territory. If you're protecting your ego, you're not showing vulnerability, so there won't be a sense of authenticity created by your words. Usually, in these situations, I will jump into the conversation and help the sales rep and myself be more vulnerable.

Say you're a couple of minutes late to a meeting. Instead of being Mr. Stuffy Superprofessional and saying, "I apologize for the delay," try saying something like, "I'm so sorry, I need to stop trusting Apple Maps instead of my own sense of direction. I've lived here my whole life!" You are likely to get a chuckle and turn the situation from "I'm inconsiderate and a bad guy for being late," into a "ha, technology fail, maybe everyone trusts apps too much." It shifts the whole tone of the meeting.

There is one big, fat disclaimer to this vulnerability thing: Your explanation has to be the *truth*. It has to be a *real* vulnerability that you're owning up to. Do not make up traffic on a major highway if that isn't the real reason you're late. Sincerity, honesty, and authenticity are all table stakes; don't mess with this. Faking vulnerability is the opposite of being authentic and will backfire—badly. If there's any hint of dishonesty in what you're saying, go home, because ain't no one gonna buy anything from you right now.

THE LANGUAGE OF ELEPHANTS

Also: don't overdo it. You don't need the customer thinking you are a scatterbrain who doesn't have your shit together. It's a fine line; be real, but don't let yourself look like a mess.

THE MASK OF ELI

I was reminded of how crucial it is to be authentic, sincere, and vulnerable in interactions with customers when I met a coaching client named Eli.

I've been working with sales professionals for a long time. It takes a lot to confound me. Eli managed to do so. He was *so stiff* it was almost intimidating. He was also uber-professional, so I couldn't get anywhere near the elephant in that guy.

I didn't enjoy talking with Eli—again, something that *rarely* happens to me when working with sales reps. Eli was confident and answered questions in a matter-of-fact way that made me want to shake him and say, "C'mon dude, can you please just be *real* for a minute?"

Without a doubt, it was the most impersonal conversation I had ever had with a sales rep. *Ever.*

Eli wasn't egotistical, he was just rigid, and wearing his professional, protective mask. His facial expressions (or lack thereof) and body language didn't help, either. I left that first meeting worried that I was going to seriously screw up the engagement. I don't typically do well with people that have such thick armor and huge walls up around them. I carried on, though, thinking this was a great opportunity for me to grow my skill set.

The second meeting completely threw me for a loop. It was as if I were speaking with a completely different person. This version of Eli was much more personable, not at all the automaton who I had met previously. He talked about his family and about how much he loved his job. He indicated he wanted to improve his ability to "connect" with others, as he knew it was holding him back.

This was the conversation that officially made me "Team Eli." He was real and vulnerable, and that just made me want to help him more. I remember that our conversation went much longer than the allotted 45-minute coaching session, and as opposed to our first conversation, I was *very* okay with that.

It was months before I had a strong enough relationship with Eli to talk to him about my personal experience with our first meeting. He had been talking about a first client meeting that he went to that didn't go very well because he felt the customer just wasn't engaging. I knew exactly why this was the case.

I used my first meeting with Eli as an example to teach him about the importance of being authentic, personable, and vulnerable. I explained to him that I suspected the customer not engaging had something to do with feeling intimidated or uncomfortable based on Eli's persona. I told Eli that customers need to see the Eli that I'd met in our second conversation, and that the first Eli I met was not going to get him very far with most customers. He understood exactly what I was saying, and he acknowledged that he was aware of his struggle with this.

We worked on this over the course of several months. I'm proud to say that Eli came a very long way. Understandably, he still backtracked to acting as the standoffish Eli when he met with someone who seemed overconfident or egotistical. That would take more time for him to get past—and I'm not sure he even needs to.

Being authentic, vulnerable, and personable is imperative to creating the types of trust relationships required to beat the bots and your competition. Get more confident with being the "real deal" when you meet with customers. If you do, I can promise you (and so can Eli) that they will much more readily engage with you and want to continue conversations with you. Not only that, but when you are vulnerable and real with your customers, they can't help but want to reciprocate. It's hard to be an egomaniac when you are dealing with someone who is humble and sincere. It makes it safe for others to trust you because they'll believe that you won't take advantage of them. Don't underestimate the power of vulnerability as you try to create customers for life.

ELEPHANT MATTERS

I was working with a sales team offering a technology solution to a large financial services company. We had spent some time building rapport and trust with the CIO, James, so that we could cautiously enter elephant territory. James was an alpha; it was more difficult to earn the right to get there. I asked, to the horror of a few of my team members, "James, where do you see your career going with this company?"

Keep in mind, I am about as real as you can get without looking like a fool (most of the time). I posed absolutely zero threat to James' ego, so it was easier for me to earn the right to ask questions on elephant matters.

James answered, "You know what? If I pull this IT transformation off, and if I'm able to show leadership that we can

use this new technology to make the business more effi-
cient, I'm going to go for the COO role—and I'd probably
have a good chance at getting it."

James wanted to be COO, a much more high-impact role
than his current position as CIO. As James was trying to tell
us, a COO has to prove that he is focused on operational efficiency. This let us know that we had to develop our proposal
and value messaging to address that business efficiency. We
would have proposed our solution very differently if we
had discovered that James wanted to be a CFO or that he
wanted to leave the company. The sales professional on the
account did an amazing job catching on to the necessary
shift in messaging that had to take place. He was able to
re-orient the entire team to speak from the same perspective and intention: to help James become the next COO.

James' company spent a lot of money flying employees
around the country for various meetings. Any time they
opened a new office anywhere in the world, they flew
a SWAT team from the home office to the new branch to
"onboard" the new advisor and staff. The SWAT team spent
a week onsite with the local team.

We were positioning a communication and collaboration
solution, including a video conferencing system that would

enable the various locations across the globe to communicate more effectively and be able to see each other on the big screen in a conference room. The sales professional, Jerry, worked with his internal business analyst and calculated that the technology solution we were proposing would reduce the time the SWAT team had to be on the road by two days, conservatively. Increasing savings and efficiency... the magic words!

We were worried that although our solution addressed the needs James had stated, it was not going to yield huge cost savings—only about 10 percent. We shared this concern with James and he set us straight. "No, guys, our issue isn't so much about the cost savings; our issue is being able to show productivity gains and increased efficiency."

Investing in our solution would show that James had a mind for efficiency and reducing travel time and expense. We won the business, and it was a huge deal for us. Six months later, James called Jerry and asked him to lunch to fill him in on his new role as COO—and said that he'd be directing the new CIO to continue working with Jerry and team on larger technology initiatives.

Recognize, though, that anyone can show cost reductions and efficiency gains. Every tech company worth its salt has templates for that. A machine can calculate these figures. What we did, though, could not have been automated. We listened carefully to James and what his goals were, and we developed and presented a solution that would help him achieve them. We put everything in the context of what we had learned about the company and James' career objectives. We were showing operational value, but we were *really* helping James become a COO. That is how we personalized value. We made his success our top priority, and each of us on the pursuit team used our unique experience and talent to add to the overall value for James.

DIFFERENTIATE AND DELIVER

Delivering personalized value doesn't always have to be about what you are selling or what goals your customer needs to achieve. You can create and deliver personalized value at any time, within the context of a specific deal or as part of strengthening an existing relationship with a client. You can do this with some simple, thoughtful acts that show you care about that customer. Let me tell you how I did this for a client named Jan.

I worked with Jan, an SVP of sales at a small IT infrastructure solutions company, as a coach for her team. The first time I met Jan, I brought these little old-school sour cherry candies. I offered one to Jan and she just loved it, so I stored that away in my memory.

When I went to meet with Jan and her team a few months later, I placed three rolls of sour cherry candies on the conference table in front of her and smiled. I didn't even have to say a word; she knew those were for her. The candies are only a little over a dollar apiece, but the look on Jan's face was priceless: surprise, appreciation, and joy. I mean, if that's not a little thing making a big impact, I don't know what is. Although this little personal exchange wasn't tied to me selling anything to Jan, it absolutely showed that I sincerely cared about her and had been paying attention to her. That was personal and the thoughtfulness helped differentiate me in Jan's mind for the long term. Even more than the exceptional results I delivered for her project could.

After my project was completed, I stayed in touch with Jan. Several months later, I got a call from her. She was with a different company and wanted me to come in and assess her new sales team to put together a plan for helping train and develop them. I thanked her for thinking of me and said I would love to work with her again. She told me, "You are the only person I want to help me clean up this mess."

Personalized value: it's the little things that go above, beyond, and to the heart that ultimately create customers for life.

In order to be thoughtful enough to differentiate, you have to know how and what your customer thinks. The only way you can earn the right to learn their thoughts is by being authentic, keeping your commitments, having integrity, and being trustworthy. Once you earn the right, you can ask questions on elephant matters.

There's no template, no checklist, no cheat sheet for creating personalized value in each of your deals. Personalized value is so unique that there's no way I can tell you exactly what it looks like. It is based on something that no one can duplicate: *you*, and what's in your head and heart. I can, though, help you learn a thought process you can use to guide you in identifying personalized value. That's what we'll look at in the next chapter.

YOUR KEY TAKEAWAY

Personalized value is the core of H2H selling and the only true way to differentiate yourself. It is a product of what you learn as you ABC the REP, a function of who you are and what you stand for, and your sincere desire and commitment to seeing your customer succeed. You can only master personalized value if you bring together these things in a way that is meaningful and relevant to your customer personally *and* in the context of their business. Earn your right with trust, gain entry to the elephant territory, and learn all you can there. Then, go do whatever it takes to get the elephant and rider moving in the direction of a favorable buying decision in the near term and customer loyalty in the long-term.

CHAPTER 7

BE AN ELEPHANT WHISPERER

Pretend that every single person you meet
has a sign around his or her neck that
says, 'Make me feel important.'

—Mary Kay Ash

'll begin this chapter with a powerful example of how to create personalized value for a customer. Then, I'll break it down into a thought process with steps that will help you learn how to become an elephant whisperer in your own right.

SOREN'S DISCOVERY

Soren was an above-average sales professional who worked hard and took care of his customers. In this scenario, he had been building trust and rapport with the CIO at a large bank for three months, and he finally earned the right to venture into elephant territory. He decided to ask the CIO, Jeremy, about his career aspirations.

Jeremy shared that he wanted to go back to school for his MBA, but he didn't feel like it was worth pursuing unless he got into a prestigious university like Northwestern. Soren could tell that Jeremy's fear of not getting into Northwestern stressed him out and was preventing him from trying to reach his goal.

Soren and Jeremy had a casual lunch one afternoon after they had gotten to know each other better; Soren summarized his company's value proposition, and Jeremy asked various questions about the proposal. Soren was confident that he had provided the requisite data and objective information to Jeremy so he could make a solid business decision—he had directed the rider, and now it was time to chat with the elephant. Soren asked Jeremy about his MBA planning, and Jeremy responded with a laugh. He indicated that he still hadn't applied for the program, but "eventually" he would.

HELP FROM A FRIEND

On his way home from lunch, Soren kept trying to think of how he could help Jeremy with his MBA plan. In brainstorming ideas, he realized that he had a connection, an old friend, that may be able to help. Soren's good friend from college, Ed, was a dean at Northwestern, but Soren wasn't sure about his exact role or duties. He immediately looked up Ed's phone number, called him, and explained that he had a friend who wanted to get in to Northwestern, but didn't feel prepared to apply and wasn't confident about his odds.

As luck would have it (as luck often does), Ed was a dean of admissions. I swear I am not making this up! Soren asked Ed if he could talk to Jeremy and answer a few questions; Ed said he'd be happy to help.

Soren called Jeremy to explain what had happened. To say that Jeremy was flabbergasted would have been an understatement; he was overwhelmed at the gesture and thanked Soren repeatedly. Soren said that he didn't know what Ed could do to help, exactly, but he would be reaching out soon. Jeremy could at least ask questions to help him better prepare his application.

A week later, Jeremy called Soren to tell him that he had spoken with Ed, and the conversation had been incredibly helpful. Ed gave him some suggestions to help improve his chances of getting in, and Jeremy had decided to apply during the next application period.

Jeremy and Soren met for lunch later that week, and Jeremy gave Soren a verbal on the multi-million-dollar deal that had been on the table. Jeremy would never openly admit that the introduction to Ed had influenced his decision, but he did say that he was overwhelmed by Soren's willingness to go out of his way to help him. He said that Soren was the kind of person he needed to work with as he transformed the bank's IT organization.

This is by far one of my favorite stories because it shows that luck favors the thoughtful and those with good intent. It is such a powerful example of differentiation through the delivery of personalized value. There is almost zero chance that a competitor could do what Soren did, and I'd also wager that Jeremy will never work with another technology sales professional ever again.

Soren was a master elephant whisperer in this sales situation. He performed the basics of company value, built rapport and trust, and directed the rider. Then, he earned the right to ask a more personal, emotionally charged question about Jeremy's career. He recognized Jeremy's personal challenge and concern with the MBA application process, and, after giving it some thought, realized that he did have a way he could help him. After Jeremy got the help he needed, it was a no-brainer for him to choose Soren's proposal for his company's IT transformation.

THE WINNING THOUGHT PROCESS

So, how can you create this type of differentiated, personal value for your customers? Let's begin by reviewing a couple of key concepts we have already established:

1. Build trust and rapport—*earn the right* to get the ticket into elephant territory.
2. Ask high-impact, elephant-centered questions— learn the motivations and emotions of your customer, and what they consider to be valuable.

Once you've done these things, the next step is to learn the thought process that ignites the spark of personalized value that only *you* can create for your customer. Again, there's no cheat sheet, but here are some questions you can ask yourself to get your creative, thoughtful ideas flowing:

*Based on what I've learned about the elephant in
my customer discovery, what are the things that
matter most to her, personally and professionally?*

The purpose of this question is to uncover tidbits of information that are unique to your customer. In Soren's case, he uncovered Jeremy's desire to apply to Northwestern's MBA program, and his fear of not getting in. That was the biggest "pain," or the most emotionally charged area for Jeremy.

Similar examples include customers who:

1. Want to improve their reputation or elevate their own image in the workplace or industry.
2. Are anxious and afraid of change because they fear that their job will be lost in the shuffle.

*What can I do to help motivate the elephant
and address the pain that was uncovered
in my discovery?*

In the example with Soren and Jeremy, the answer wasn't immediately obvious. Soren had to go through the process of thinking about how he could create personalized value. In that process, Soren realized there was someone in his network that he could ask for a favor. He had a resource that could help him create personalized value.

For a customer who is extremely preoccupied with their own reputation or personal brand, ask yourself how you can feed into that. You might ask that customer if they would like to be a guest star on your company's new technology-focused podcast, if they are available to speak at an upcoming event, or if they are willing to do a guest blog post. You can do something as simple as "like" their posts on LinkedIn, comment on why their posts are valuable, and share them with your network. If you are able to bring even one of these ideas to fruition, you will deliver personalized value by targeting precisely what the elephant has indicated is a motivator.

In the case of a client who is extremely risk-averse and has an overwhelming fear of change, you can find ways to shift their perception of the risk associated with the sale you are trying to make. If you have a customer who was once an "anxious Andy" about partnering with you and your company, but is now a raving fan, you can use that unique past relationship to your advantage. You could contact your raving-fan client and ask them to speak to your anxious prospect—they can share how well things turned out for them after they partnered with you.

What are my options for personalizing value,
and which one will be the most impactful?

Once you narrow it down to a few ideas on how you can create personalized value, you have to choose the most meaningful, powerful, and compelling one in the context of your sales situation, and your comfort level with the customer.

In Soren's case, he zeroed in on the piece of information about Jeremy wanting to go to business school. At first, he thought about sending Jeremy some articles that had insight on the application process; he even found a book he thought that Jeremy would be interested in reading, but neither of those gestures felt extraordinary. Once he remembered Ed, he knew that creating a connection between him and Jeremy would be the most valuable thing he could do for Jeremy.

Can anybody else do it?

The most effective personalized value comes from providing something that nobody else can. In Soren's case, sending an article would not have been nearly as valuable, because anyone could have done that. Even if there was tailored messaging within the content, it still wouldn't have been a very personal or unique gesture. Only Soren had a relationship with both the dean and Jeremy, so he was the only one who was able to connect them. Soren leveraged who he knew in a powerful way to deliver personalized value, which is precisely what H2H is all about. High performing sales reps learn how to leverage any and all resources they have access to. They take the time to think through how they can use their resources to help their customers achieve their goals. Personalizing value transforms sales professionals into purveyors of value. This is the stuff that can knock a bot out of the picture.

Where are we in our relationship, and is my strategy appropriate at this time?

When evaluating where you are in your relationship, it's important to look at *the value of the interactions*, rather than the amount of time that has passed. How much rapport-building have you done? How much trust have you created? Have you made a strong enough connection to provide personalized value on a deeper, more meaningful level? If you have learned about the customer's unique personal and professional needs, I hope that you have already done this. If you haven't, you need to be mindful of the activities you are creating around personal value—make sure they are appropriate for that point in the relationship.

I have seen some sales professionals create a meaningful connection and a remarkable amount of trust in as little as one meeting! Others, however, may work with a customer for months, and a gesture of personalized value may seem over the top and possibly manipulative because the relationship has yet to develop. If you are in this situation and you think you have a great idea for personal value, don't act on it until you know it is appropriate for the nature of the relationship. Remember, you have to earn the right to play in personalized-value, elephant territory.

This concept is a little more difficult to get right, so let's go back to the example of Soren and Jeremy. Imagine that Soren had learned about Jeremy's MBA goal during their first or second meeting. If he had immediately taken that information and asked Ed for the favor, Jeremy most likely would have been grateful, but he also would have found it strange that Soren was getting that personal so soon. He may have perceived it as a sales play, or that Soren was trying to gain his business through other means.

How will my personalized value be perceived?

If you were able to answer the previous questions without issue, your customer will likely appreciate the personalized value that you choose to deliver. However, I strongly advise you to take a moment to think about how your customer will perceive your actions. Just because something seems like a great idea and you think it will create differentiated, personalized value, it doesn't always mean that your customer will—you have to think about it from their perspective.

Once you believe that your customer will value your action and intent, you can move forward. You are likely to succeed, and in addition, your organization will view your approach in a positive light because it was differentiated and probably landed you the deal.

Is my idea of personalized value creepy?

This is often related to timing, as I mentioned above. Something that may be creepy to ask or do during a first meeting won't necessarily be creepy after working with a customer for six months.

Let's say you see a Chicago Cubs pennant on a customer's wall when you first meet them in their office, but you don't get a chance to ask about it. If you think that giving the customer a pair of tickets to a Cubs game would be a great way to create some personalized connection and value, slow your roll. That would be creepy. You've only known him for a minute, and you never even talked about the Cubs, so you really have no idea if he is a big fan. You haven't built up enough knowledge, trust, or rapport to get a ticket into elephant territory. Doing something like this will come off as creepy, slimy, and sneaky. Nope, nope and nope.

However, if you've known this customer for months, you are safely in elephant territory, and you learn that you are both huge Cubs fans who typically hit the same bar before a game, then it's a great idea to get tickets to an upcoming game and invite the customer along. You can even make sure you go to that bar you both like. This is a small act of personalized value that is not creepy, because camaraderie and rapport were built on the foundation of your mutual love for the Cubs.

Now, let me tell you about a scenario that is straight up creepy. I get the heebie-jeebies just thinking about it. I once worked with a sales professional, Dan, who learned from one of his friends that a top prospect of his, Luis, was the coach for a soccer team in the same district as his daughter's. Dan's daughter was in the right age bracket for Luis' soccer team, so he decided to enroll her on Luis' team as a means to learn more about him and strengthen their relationship.

Dan attended every single game and made it a point to always talk to Luis trying to create a more personal relationship. That's creepy as hell. And don't think that Luis didn't know what Dan was doing. The friend who told Dan about Luis' being a coach later told Dan that Luis felt his behavior was "stalkerish," and couldn't understand why Dan would use his daughter as part of his sales strategy. Luis was cordial to Dan, but he would never buy anything from him—he thought he was wacko. To be fair, Dan wasn't a creep or a wacko, and he wasn't trying to be manipulative; he just hadn't given much thought to his grand plan for personalized value. Unfortunately, he learned an important lesson the hard way.

It would have been far less creepy if Luis had volunteered the information about being a coach and said that his team was looking for additional players. Then, Dan could have volunteered his daughter. The way that Dan did things was not OK. If Dan had simply thought, "How will this make Luis feel?" he would likely have figured out that his plan was not a good idea and would probably backfire.

Is it unethical?

It was completely ethical for Soren to connect Jeremy and Ed because it was done with good intent for Jeremy's benefit. He was simply connecting two individuals in order to exchange some important information.

An example of an absolutely unethical strategy I have seen is "poaching" a customer to come work for your company. In one particular scenario, Evan, a sales professional I worked with, had a customer who was frustrated with her role as IT Director. She had reached out to Evan and asked him to help her find a job at his company, maybe even give her a referral. Evan called me and asked how to handle the situation. He thought that putting in a good word would differentiate himself in the eyes of this prospect, who would still have plenty of time to sign a sizeable deal before she got called for an interview. Um...*nope*.

I had to help Evan see that no good would come from this situation. Before we even get into non-competes or other contractual agreements between B2Bs, it's just plain unethical to engage in a quid-pro-quo situation such as this. It isn't even a "gray area"; it's pretty black and white. *You don't poach from customers.*

I told Evan to forget about it. Not only was it highly unethical, but it was also a sales suicide mission. His company would likely have to reject that customer for contractual reasons, and she would be upset that he wasn't able to come through for her. He'd likely never sign anything with that customer again. If she ended up leaving her company, how likely would it be for her boss to meet with Evan in the future, given that he tried to steal an employee? The word would get out that you tried to hire one of your customers, and a shitstorm would surely follow. Nobody has time for that.

What's my best strategy for delivering personalized value to the right person?

You must always, always, ask yourself if you have earned enough trust and asked enough of the right questions to create the most effective, personalized value proposition. Once you know that you have the right strategy, you must be thoughtful in the execution. When dealing with personal, elephant matters, there's much room for even the best intentions to pave the road to "deal hell."

Soren's effort with Jeremy worked because it was appropriate given the level of trust between them. It was the best-case scenario for personalized value. And because Soren got the right information and asked the right questions, it set him up to ink a successful deal.

However, it's not always that easy. The customer may be much harder to move, or you may encounter someone who blocks your efforts. For example, I recently worked with a remarkable sales team that was trying to sell a solution to a small bank. The IT leader and gatekeeper, Bob, was quite resistant to working with anyone outside of his organization; he wanted to keep all technology services in house and under his control. He just wanted to deal in transactional exchanges, such as simple product purchases. This set Alyssa, the sales professional, and her pursuit team on a mission to show the bank how much value they could bring with their broad portfolio of technology products and solutions. To do that, the team needed to get past Bob, the server-hugger-gatekeeper, and reach a more strategic, c-level contact.

In typical "level selling 101" form, the sales team tried to broker a meeting between their company's CEO, Andrew, and the CEO of the small, community bank, Emilio. Not surprisingly, Bob kept declining on Emilio's behalf. From a cultural standpoint, the team knew they were being sabotaged, because one small-business CEO in this community would never be so dismissive of another. That world was just too small.

The sales team continued to brainstorm how to get around Bob. They realized that Emilio was an avid, obsessive golfer. Andrew was, as well, so Alyssa set up the two CEOs for a round of golf at the most elite course in the area. That way, they could get the leaders to talk without Bob blocking them.

It worked. Emilio appreciated the direct invite from Andrew and was very impressed with what he learned about the company. He decided to advise Bob to look more carefully at the solutions they had proposed.

That is how you do personalized value *at the right level*. This sales team could have tried for months to find ways to create personalized value in the eyes of the gatekeeper, but Bob was never going to change—he'd never allow them into elephant territory. Since there was no practical way to motivate the gatekeeper's elephant, the team had to think more strategically. They recognized that they needed to focus on creating value for the c-level executive, Emilio, instead of the sabotaging-server-hugger.

It takes practice, but if you commit to being mindful about personalized value, ask customers the right questions to create it, and deliver at the appropriate time, I promise you will see a remarkable shift in your sales interactions and results. Becoming an elephant whisperer is how you win big today, create customers for life, and beat the bots.

YOUR KEY TAKEAWAY

To become an elephant whisperer, you must recognize how crucial it is to address the emotional system of the buyer's mind. You earn your ticket into elephant territory and the right to whisper by establishing rapport, trust, and connection.

You have to get the relevant personal information—the stuff that really matters to customers and will motivate them to change—by asking the right questions, and then transforming what you learn into personalized value. There is no cheat sheet on how to create this because it is based on the unique H2H interaction between the buyer and seller. There is, however, a series of questions you can ask yourself to discover potential options and to help you identify which ones are most compelling. Figure out the right person to connect with, create your personalized value strategy, and then ascertain the best way to execute. But don't even think about getting creepy. Creepy never wins.

CHAPTER 8

WHEN THE INK DRIES

Loyal customers, they don't just come back,
they don't simply recommend you, they insist
that their friends do business with you.

—Chip Bell

e've mentioned how important it is to create and deliver personalized value throughout the sales cycle. To create customers for life, personalized value isn't something that you focus on only during the pursuit; you have to commit to creating and delivering value throughout the entire customer engagement. This includes pre-sale, the time following the sale, and for as long as you both shall live. Kidding. Sort of.

You must listen, care, and deliver personalized value beyond the close of a deal—this is simply what the best reps do. They recognize that helping clients succeed consists of more than a series of efforts to get to ink; it's an ongoing responsibility to deliver unique value, and it has to continue throughout the duration of the relationship. This is why so many companies heavily invest in "customer success" teams today.

AFTER THE SALE

In a technology sale, there's typically some sort of an implementation or onboarding process where the customer transitions from their current technology to the solution they purchased from you. You have to stay close to the client during this transition because it's the first real experience they will have with your company post-sale. You have the ultimate opportunity to prevent buyer's remorse and ensure that the customer does not feel like they are "out of sight, out of mind."

Think of how disappointed the customer would be if you

handed them off to some other team member in your organization after they've grown accustomed to you and the personalized value you have delivered during the sales process. Sadly, technology organizations and sales professionals botch this handoff all the time.

In my experience, after a deal is closed, the sales professional and an executive take the customers out for dinner and thank them for their business; they toast to a long, fruitful relationship or something equally meaningless. Then, they pass the customers on to an implementation team. Frequently, salespeople do this through an e-mail to their customer: "Liam is your implementation specialist, and he'll be working with you throughout this process. Please reach out to him with any questions or concerns you may have." Cold, right? Yep, but I can't tell you how many times I have seen this happen. Facepalm after facepalm after facepalm.

The above example is *not* what elephant whisperers do. High performers set up a lunch or another face-to-face meeting with their customer and the implementation specialist. Those high performers make damn sure that the specialist understands key information from the sales cycle: what the customer finds valuable, and the value they've personally created along the way. Transitioning in this manner drastically reduces the chances of the implementation falling off the rails, and assures the customer that they will be well cared for throughout the process.

A face-to-face handoff more like this would change the game: "Hey, this is Liam. He's your guy. He'll take care of you and make sure there aren't any hiccups along the way. I've told him all the things we've talked about. Don't hesitate to call him, or me, if you need anything." Then Liam would say something like "Yeah, absolutely. Here's my cellphone number."

The customer is far less likely to bitch about Liam in this case, given that the sales professional whom they trust has personally vouched for him. That's the "warm fuzzy" effect that exceptional sales professionals recognize as being essential every step of the way.

I'd like to think that this goes without saying, but I know it can't. Even if a customer loves their new post-sales contact, you have to remain close throughout the implementation. If there are regular check-in calls during the process, you should be on them, or at the very least, send e-mails to your customer and inquire about how things are going. Make sure that the transition team keeps you in the loop so you can jump in anytime the standard of performance is lower than the one you have set. Remember, the goal is to have customers for life who don't want to work with anyone or anything else. You can't achieve that if you disengage when the ink dries and the commission check is cashed.

PROVIDING RELIEF

Sharon was a medical device sales professional who had recently sold her device to a hospital called St. Augustine's. The device allowed nurses to run blood tests more efficiently, and to obtain results more quickly, making it particularly valuable to hospital emergency departments (EDS). There was some initial basic training that an ED employee—typically the Director—had to go through so they could later train all of the nurses.

Florence, the ED Director, was extremely anxious about delivering this training. She was a nurse, so she wasn't concerned that she would struggle with learning how to use the device—something much bigger and more personal bothered her. Florence had moved to the United States from the Philippines over two decades ago, but she still had a pretty thick accent when she spoke. She was mortified at the idea of delivering training and was convinced that the audience wouldn't be able to understand her. The fear of embarrassment caused Florence to keep postponing her onboarding.

Sharon recognized that Florence was apprehensive about delivering the training by asking her several thoughtful, high impact questions. Sharon recognized an opportunity to go above and beyond to deliver personalized value to the elephant, and consequentially, to the hospital.

Sharon asked Florence if it would be helpful if she delivered the training for her. She made this offer without indicating that she recognized Florence's fear and insecurity—she was kind enough to know that it wasn't necessary. Florence was thrilled and grateful, and she even bought Sharon a box of chocolates to thank her.

Sharon had already sold the product, so there was no commission check coming from this action; she did it because it was the right thing to do. In addition, this H2H interaction made a lasting impression on Florence. We'll talk more about that later.

AFTER THE IMPLEMENTATION

Make no mistake about this: after the technology has been implemented and your company is regularly managing the customer, the need for personalized value still exists. You still need to follow up with your customer and ask questions like, "Hey, how are things going? What's changed? How's the business doing?"

This is much easier to do if you're the original salesperson. If you're an account manager, or "farmer," it takes some time to build rapport and trust. Of course, you'll have a head start because the original sales rep will have personally vouched for you. To build the relationship, however, you must consistently check on the customer and ask questions; find new opportunities to create personalized value. Top performers, hunters and farmers alike, realize that their efforts must persist after the sale to protect revenue, pursue account expansion, and ensure renewal. You are always in a sales cycle.

QUARTERLY BUSINESS REVIEW

The quarterly business review (QBR) between the sales and account team and the customer stakeholders is regarded by many customers as a way to micromanage service delivery. It should not be. If you do QBRs right, they can become one big fat sales opportunity. QBRs provide a way to strengthen emotional connections and uncover opportunities to help you continually differentiate. It's a great chance to offer insight to customers, share articles, or talk about the newest technology.

There is, of course, the matter of the service review in the QBR. Smart salespeople make sure well in advance that the SLAS are being met, and that the customer is happy. In order for the QBR to be an opportunity to sell and strengthen relationships, you have to ensure it is not a service-issue bitching session. I've found that the best account managers conduct weekly or monthly meetings with their clients to address service-related issues, so by the time the QBR rolls around, there is nothing left to bitch about. This turns the QBR into an advisory conversation, giving you a chance to provide proactive guidance and insight—this shows the customer that you have their best interests at heart. It can be something simple like: "Based on how we see your users adapting to the technology, we think it might be a good idea for you to create a job aid to better communicate the instructions to them."

You can also ask questions such as: "You have a new CTO, what is his vision? What's he thinking? How's your life going to change?" Or, "I see you've just acquired these two companies. What does that mean for your IT infrastructure? How are you going to integrate? Oh, you mean you need to buy twenty more servers?" Cha-ching! Continuing to ask high-impact questions throughout steady-state business is the key to uncovering opportunities to increase wallet share.

QBRS are also instrumental in making renewals a no-brainer. You become such a valuable advisor and coach that your customer can't fathom *not* renewing. I mean, who else will always be in their corner? QBRS make renewals effortless because your value is so clearly established, and ideally, renewal conversations will become non-events.

LASTING IMPACT

Remember Sharon, the medical device sales rep who delivered the training for Florence? She didn't believe that dry ink meant she could walk away and forget about delivering personalized value. In fact, the value she delivered was deeply personal and helped to alleviate a major fear and insecurity for her customer. No one else could have done that.

A few months after she delivered that training, Sharon received a voicemail from a hospital administrator named Jared, who led a group of hospitals in her region. He said that he was interested in learning about the ED testing devices she sold.

Sharon was confounded by that message. She had called on that hospital group a few times before, but no one had ever called her back. She knew that she hadn't called anyone named Jared, before. Her mind raced as she tried to figure out how this man had found her. She wanted to at least have some idea about him before she called him back.

She did some research to look for connections, but she couldn't find any. She gave up on trying to figure it out, and she called him back. He thanked her for calling and explained that his Aunt Florence, the nursing director at St. Augustine's Hospital, had told him what Sharon had done for her. She had also told Jared how well her ED nurses were doing with the new devices, and the positive outcomes they already had in terms of patient satisfaction. Florence asked him to reach out to Sharon to determine if his hospital group could benefit from the devices.

Jared signed a multi-million-dollar deal with Sharon a few short months later.

Yep, that happened.

It happened because Sharon differentiated herself to Florence in a way that no one else could have, at a deeply personal level. Her action led to a referral with an even bigger commission check (roughly three times bigger, if you must know).

Personalized value reaches people at a level that little else can—it creates a deep sense of respect and loyalty. When you become an elephant whisperer and master the art of differentiating through personalized value, you create customers for life, and they are a gift that keeps on giving.

YOUR KEY TAKEAWAY

Closing a deal doesn't mean that you can walk away or quit after the personalized value delivery. The art of identifying and delivering personalized value continues well after the ink dries on an initial contract. Keep asking questions and finding ways to do things that matter to your customers; make them realize that you are an invaluable advocate for their success, and you are in it for the long haul. How you behave after the deal is done will influence the customer's loyalty, improve your ability to expand in the account, and turn renewals into no brainers.

It's important to understand that the more personalized value you deliver in ongoing interactions, the more you will matter to the customer. They will continue to trust you and seek your counsel - they will continually want to do business with you, regardless of what company you work for, or even what you are selling. Personalized value creates customers for life, and customers for life become advocates for your success who love to send referrals your way. Customers that need you and genuinely want you to succeed will help ensure you are not replaced by a competitor or a machine.

CHAPTER 9

SURVIVAL OF THE DEAREST

*First, delighting customers doesn't build
loyalty; reducing their effort—the work they
must do to get their problem solved—does.*
—Matthew Dixon, Karen Freeman,
and Nicholas Toman

Being delightful is just "good enough," but I want you to be *more* than good enough; I want you to be indispensable.

One of my newer coaching clients, Sam, called to tell me about closing a sizable tech services deal. He was very excited about how he had differentiated himself and delighted the customer, saying that he felt he was absolutely their trusted advisor and strategic partner now. I, of course, responded with, "Yay, you!"

My heart swells with pride every time I get one of these calls. However, the more I listened to Sam talk about what a great experience the customer had, the more I realized that he had missed some of the important nuances about customer experience. He didn't understand the full picture of what personalized value is and what it does. We had talked about creating value and personalizing experiences throughout the customer's buying journey. We discussed making sure that the presales experience was delightful for customers. God love him, he had gone and done just that: delighted his customer in the process of closing this big deal.

"The process of closing this big deal." Say it out loud. It sounds like a one-and-done sort of thing, right? It feels finite. I needed Sam to understand an important detail that makes a huge difference in terms of shaping your performance and the customer's perception: creating a delightful experience is not enough to differentiate you in the long term.

CLEO THE DELIGHTFUL

So, what is the difference between delight and endearment? Let's look at a specific example of an experience that was delightful.

Last year, my family decided to do a summer "staycation" at a hotel called EMC2 in downtown Chicago. The hotel's theme was sort of modern steampunk or industrial chic, which made it look great. The coolest part, though, was that the hotel had two real, functional robots, named Cleo and Leo, that could interact with guests (they were pretty fantastic, so I can't call them bots. Remember, that's the word for the evil ones—Cleo and Leo were cute). The robots were about three feet tall, had small screens to communicate messages, and they could deliver any small thing you needed to your room. These robots were *so* intriguing that even my aloof, too-cool teenagers were mesmerized.

Of course, we had to see the robots in action, so we used an app on the TV to order some shampoo. As soon as the order was placed, the kids ran into the hallway with their phones to document the adventure. They were so excited about the experience that they fought over who would take the video and who would take photos for Instagram (or Snapchat, or whatever the app-of-the-day was). A few minutes later, Cleo was at our room door, and her little screen gave us instructions on how to get the shampoo out of the compartment at the top. We lifted the lid, got our shampoo, and Cleo took her leave from us—but not until she confirmed that we had what we needed.

Cleo delighted us and the other hotel guests, her customers. She created a memorable experience. While writing this, I asked my kids the name of the robots and they immediately told me, adding, "That was the coolest thing." *That* was an experience. It was delightful. And it's over now. Sure, we remember the robot delivery, but it wasn't meaningful enough for us to go back to that hotel again. Hell, it wasn't even compelling enough to keep us from bitching about how much we paid to valet the car—*that* was criminal.

Again, a delightful experience isn't enough.

I want you to be *more than enough*.

I want you to become the be-all-end-all guide, coach, and problem solver for your customers. I think you can be the person they never forget, the one they come back to time and time again, regardless of where you or they work. I want them to be delighted by not just the experience: I want you to endear yourself to them so that they know that every experience with you will be a delight.

When you delight your customers, you do so for a period of time, but time passes and the powerful feeling of that moment goes with it. When you endear yourself to your customers, you create a more lasting impression. Delight is about experience; endearment is about *you*. A delightful experience can be imitated. A sales professional who has endeared themselves to a customer is inimitable. That sales professional will differentiate and, inevitably, beat the bots and the competition.

Don't just focus on delighting your customer; make it your mission to endear yourself to your customer. You become dear to them by consistently creating and delivering personalized value and remarkable, delightful experiences. Endearing is a process through which you become "their person." That's a role no robot can play. It's a nightmare for even the fiercest competitor to try to unseat you from an account where you have endeared yourself to the client.

When you personalize a customer's experience and delight your customer through a sales cycle, they will remember you for it. When you repeatedly serve and delight them with personalized value, they won't want to buy from anyone else—and you may even find your customers going out of their way to protect you when the competition comes along. That's just what you do for people you hold dear.

DEAR DIGICOM

Hayley, one of my favorite coaching clients, is the perfect example of someone who consistently delivers personalized value across delightful experiences and, as a result, endears herself to her customers.

Hayley was one of the newer reps at her IT services company, Digicom. She had incredible energy and was just fun to be around. Because she cared *a lot* about her customers and helping them succeed, she formed meaningful, trusting relationships with them.

As we discussed who she could reach out to in her network that would benefit from the solutions Digicom had to offer, she told me about Becky, a previous client who had recently made a huge career leap into a CIO role at a large manufacturing company. Hayley said she had a "pretty good" relationship with Becky, but once she explained some of her previous deals it sounded like Hayley had gone above and beyond with personalized value to endear herself to Becky. I said she should absolutely reach out to Becky, but Hayley was hesitant. She mentioned how different Digicom's products were from the solutions she had previously sold to Becky. She was concerned that her relationship wasn't strong enough for Becky to be interested in hearing about Digicom.

I kept pushing (I know, shocking). I told Hayley that she had differentiated herself as a partner for Becky, and Becky would remember what Hayley had done to help her succeed in her previous role. My persistent nudging worked. Hayley finally called Becky, and it went exceptionally well. Next thing I knew, Hayley had booked Becky to come into the Digicom corporate office for a tour and executive meeting. Within a few months, Hayley had three deals on the table with Becky's corporation—big ones!

One day shortly thereafter, Becky called Hayley and told her that she had been working with a technology manufacturer who had partnered with one of Digicom's competitors and that the sales rep was...*unremarkable* (I won't use the words she used).

Becky went on: "I reached out to the manufacturer and told them that if they want my business, they need to partner with Digicom so I can work with you."

I told Haley that she should be really proud of this. She had been such a strong customer advocate for Becky that her customer was now an advocate for her, as well. What Becky had done for Hayley is something you would do for someone you hold dear.

One of the telltale signs of a rep who has mastered the art of delivering personalized value and endeared herself to the customer is when the customer protects the rep's interests and seeks out opportunities for her. Delight is about experiences, about what you do—it's just one thing that top sales professionals do. It's not enough, however. Endearment is about people, about who you are and how you've made a difference at an H2H level with your customer. And it is so much more than enough.

TEST YOURSELF

Once you have endeared yourself to the customer, you change the entire dynamic of the relationship and can begin to enjoy the benefits of the powerful new dynamic. Endearment, however, isn't a switch that gets flipped at a certain point. It's something that happens over time, across various interactions between sales rep and client. How do you know, though, that you have actually endeared yourself to the customer?

There are a series of questions you can ask yourself to help you recognize the nature of your relationship with the customer and if you can truly say that you have endeared yourself to them. Take a look at the list of questions below. You can use these to help you determine if you've truly become dear to your client, or if there's more work to be done.

1. Will they miss me when I'm gone? Why?

2. If my sales manager called them for a meeting to gather feedback on my performance, what would my customers tell him?

3. Do they typically call or text me back right away when I reach out to them?

4. Would they readily refer me to their peers or other contacts?

5. Are they on time for my meetings?

6. Do they fight hard to negotiate down the pricing?

7. Do they reach out to me to provide information that is relevant in their context?

8. Do they typically ask me for my opinion when they are making decisions?

9. Would they be willing to promote my company via a customer testimonial or video, or by agreeing to speak about the work we've done together at an upcoming event?

10. Do they do things for me that help me be more successful?

It's important that you don't take for granted that you've endeared yourself to your customer based on your "gut instinct." I don't care how good you feel your instinct is, find ways to make sure that you are seeing the situation objectively enough to know the difference.

Don't let anyone make you think that delighting your customer is enough. It's not. Endear yourself to the customer through consistent delivery of value and keep an eye on their behaviors to see how well your efforts are working.

Delight is finite; endearment lasts. Delight is about experiences, but endearment is about *you*, and what you mean to the customer. Strive to endear yourself to customers knowing that you will delight them in the process.

Now you know better...and I know that you'll do better, because of it.

YOUR KEY TAKEAWAY

To beat the bots, to future-proof your career, you have to strive for endearment. Delighting customers has become table stakes. Everyone and their mother goes on and on about creating a delightful customer experience. It's in ads, sales trainings, social media, and marketing. It's common. But endearment endures where delight disappears. Endearment is remarkable. Strive for remarkable and endear yourself to your customers through consistently creating and delivering personalized value, before the sale, during implementation, and throughout your happily ever after.

CHAPTER 10

A BRAND IS BORN

If you are not a brand, you are a commodity.

—Robert Kiyosaki

I seriously think my friend Joe knows everybody worth knowing. Whenever I have a problem—anything from fixing the plumbing in my house to revamping my website—I call Joe. He always says something like, "Oh, I have a guy for that. Let me give you his number." Joe is a loyal soul, and his standards are high. When he makes a recommendation, I know his "guy" will deliver and be well worth the price. Unless they are too far away or we have some other logistical challenge, I *always* go with the people Joe knows.

I want you to be the Joe of b2b sales professionals.

I am fortunate enough to be this trusted person for my customers. I have been in business for myself since 2014, and I am proud and humbled to say that all of my customers to date have come to me through referrals. The most incredible part is that these referred customers keep me so busy that many times I've had to turn away new business or schedule projects a few months out. In a million years, I never could have imagined that I'd be so blessed.

BUILD YOUR AUTHENTIC BRAND

In my business, I practice everything I've shared with you in this book, and I've cultivated my own brand because of it. My brand has become trusted and it means partnership, emotional acumen, and psychology in sales. I have become known as the "Elephant Whisperer" and the person who gifts plush elephants to her clients so they never forget how important it is to appeal to people at an emotional level.

Yes, my company itself is a brand, but my service and care for clients have made Anita Nielsen a brand. The h2h interaction that comes from having a personal brand is so much more powerful than all the things that companies try to do to engage with customers. Company brands can't reach the level of loyalty that you can at an H2H level when you have built your own personal brand identity.

Now it's your turn to discover and build your brand.

As you get better at integrating the principles of personalized value into your sales motion, your personal brand identity will naturally emerge. It's cumulative, getting more powerful and better defined the more H2H relationships you cultivate. And though you may not recognize it initially, I can promise that your customers will. They will create a perception of you and the way you do business. That perception, which essentially becomes your personal brand, revolves around who you are, what you stand for, and the partnership you create throughout your H2H relationship with that customer. They will be loyal to your brand regardless of where their career takes them because you are trusted, you are their person. They see that no one else can do for them exactly what you do, the way you do it.

Authenticity is intertwined with your ability to create a powerful, memorable, personal brand. An authentic brand is one that people trust. It helps people feel safe because they know they are in the presence of someone who is *real and vulnerable*. When you lead with sincerity and vulnerability, who you are and what you stand for, truly, will be one of the most endearing things about you in the minds of your customers. Customers want to know what they are getting; they need to know that the person that they are entrusting with their money—and often their reputation—is genuine.

Authenticity is a prerequisite to ensure the brand that emerges from your efforts is one that you and your customers can be proud of. Without authenticity, not only will you be unable to whisper to elephants, you'll fail to differentiate. There are too many self-serving sellers still out there, sadly, and if a customer senses that you are not being real, you will become obsolete. You'll be doing shots with Leisure Suit Larry in a gross dive bar before you know it.

NEIL'S BIG DEAL

As your authentic brand identity emerges from delivering personalized value to your customers, you will benefit from deep loyalty. Not only will customers be loyal to you, but they will also happily refer you and your services to others.

Remember Neil, from the preface of this book? I have had the pleasure of coaching Neil and celebrating his wins with him over the course of a few years. He's the kind of client you dream about because he is willing to do the hard work to shift his mindset and actions in order to elevate himself and his sales career. Recently, Neil worked on a complex, large deal with an insurance company throughout which, with coaching, he became a master of personalized value. He won the deal, of course—and the *monster* commission check that came along with it.

Because I am always looking for stories and examples to share with other reps, I asked Neil if I could ask his customer champion, Tom the CIO, about his experience with Neil. Neil had already earned the right to ask this of Tom, as his relationship was built on trust and mutual respect. Neil set up my conversation with Tom and it is one I will never forget.

I asked Tom, "You had three vendors trying to win this business from you. Why did you choose to award the business to Neil?"

"Look," he replied, "in the past, when we needed to buy some equipment, we had a bunch of vendors that we called for quotes and we'd pick and choose what we needed based on the price. A few times I even approved technology purchases direct from CDW. I realized, though, that I need to work with someone who can help me figure out what I need to be buying in the first place. Someone who can help me keep up with all the shit going on at this company and with our competitors. Neil has my back; he is always trying to make me look good."

I pressed Tom for more. "How does he do that?"

"I can call him anytime to help me figure out what I need to do or to help me get shit off the fan. I trust that he'll help me handle whatever IT related problems I have. The fact that I always kick his ass on the golf course is a bonus."

I chuckled and I'm sure my joy showed on my face. "I get it. He's pretty great—not that I'm biased or anything!"

Let me tell you, this is the kind of conversation coaches *live* for. I left that meeting overwhelmed with pride, and there may or may not have been some tears when I got back to the car. Neil's brand identity had emerged as an advisor and fixer for IT leaders. Not the Ray Donovan kind, but a strategic, business-partner sort of fixer. They counted on him for proactive and reactive support in their business. But it didn't stop there.

A few months later, Tom referred another CIO from his peer group to Neil, to address an issue similar to those Neil had resolved for him. In fact, within a year of closing that first deal, Neil had gotten four referrals from Tom. One of these wasn't a good fit due to the size of the company; two are currently in progress and will be closed by the time you read this book; and the last one resulted in a multimillion-dollar, five-year contract—the largest deal of the year for Neil's company.

Beyond that, Neil's wife did not have to go back to work and, at this rate, will likely never need to. They have moved into their dream house, and have put their kids into the top private school in the region. Most importantly, Neil no longer feels like he is always in a pressure cooker. He enjoys knowing that his work has a positive impact on the people he serves. His boss uses Neil as an example for other reps to learn from and gives Neil a great deal of control over his business. Neil is happier, excited about what he does, and he knows that he is going to be okay. In fact, he is better than okay; he is unstoppable.

The bonus for me is that, because Neil was kicking ass so hard, his company asked me to begin coaching additional sales professionals on Neil's team. This gave me the opportunity to convert a whole new group of reps into masters of personalized value, who can differentiate themselves and future-proof their B2B tech sales careers.

Neil's shiny new brand identity actually put some polish on my personal brand, as well.

THE FIRE IN YOUR BELLY

You are a million different things. But there's something unique about you that will be valuable in the context of your interactions with every single customer. It's on you to figure out what that is by using the techniques you've learned in this book.

You can get a head start, though, with some self-awareness. (I told you my background is in psychology; did you seriously think you were going to get through this book without a little soul searching?) Think about what makes you uniquely *you*. What's the fire in your belly that drives you to differentiate yourself? Asking this and the questions below will help you determine what types of personalized value are best for you to start with.

QUESTIONS FOR SELF-REFLECTION

- What can I do for clients that no other sales professionals do?
- What do I believe in that will help customers believe in me?
- How can I help my customers feel like I want to

collaborate with them to help them succeed?

- How can I get comfortable with being real, sincere, and vulnerable in my customer interactions?
- What are my favorite questions to ask customers, to figure out what matters most to them?
- How will I recognize when something I want to do for the customer may come off as creepy?
- What types of resources do I have at my disposal that I can leverage to help customers in the context of what I sell?
- And here's the biggie: *Why should they buy from me?*

No one else should be able to give the same answer you did for this last question. Your answer here will become the foundation for your personal brand. Be very thoughtful and deliberate about your answer.

LOOKING FOR THE MOTHER LODE

Big deal after big deal, as you deliver personalized value and care deeply about your customers' success, your brand identity will emerge. Continue to hone your craft and strive to establish a reputation for being genuine, trustworthy, knowledgeable, connected, and resourceful. Work to make sure your customers know that if you can't answer their question, you'll take ownership of finding someone who can. Give them confidence that you'll always help them find a solution or resolution.

When you do, your customers will become walking advertisements for you. They'll recommend you to their peers. If the buying decision at their own company is in hands other than theirs, they will be your advocate and help gain consensus around the solution you are selling. When you become your customers' biggest advocate for success, they will become yours. And that, my dears, is when you know you have hit the mother lode.

YOUR KEY TAKEAWAY

The more meaningful H2H interactions you have with customers where you endear yourself to them, the more you will shape your own personal brand identity. Continually work on improving your brand. Having a personal brand doesn't just matter to your job today; it ensures the long-term sustainability of a highly successful career as a top performer. Your personal brand is one of the most powerful weapons you can use to beat the bots.

CONCLUSION

BUH-BYE, LEISURE SUIT LARRY

If the Leisure Suit Larrys of the world, the slimy, sneaky, shady sales guys, aren't extinct yet, they soon will be. The internet has empowered and educated buyers so that they no longer need sales professionals for information. Buyers crave a new kind of sales professional, someone who doesn't want to "sell" them, but who wants to help them succeed. I believe you can be that someone.

As sales professionals, it's easy to get caught up and want to close a deal as quickly as possible when a customer is excited about a shiny new technology. But technology is only as good as the value it creates for the business. The key is to remember that selling them a shiny new technology won't differentiate you. How you help make that technology shine for your customers' business will. If you can be the person to help your customer make that technology matter in the context of their organization, you differentiate yourself and, over time, help eliminate the perception about salespeople being "slimy, sneaky, and shady."

Technology is no joke. Advances in artificial intelligence, machine learning, and robotics are increasingly a threat to B2B sales professionals. It's more important than ever that sales professionals work on sharpening their sales skills, especially the ability to uncover and articulate differentiating value to customers.

The thing is, most sales professionals have precious little left that they can use to differentiate—but you have everything you need to win any deal. It's in you. It's a function of you. What will make you successful is who you are, what you stand for, and what you're willing to do for your unique customer. If you learn to win customers' trust, differentiate yourself, provide them value that matters and sets them up to succeed, you will never lose your B2B tech sales job to a website or robot. You will become a master of the most powerful form of selling, Human to Human. A human thoughtfully and empathetically uses high-impact questions, active listening, and psychology to help create connection and trust at a level a robot never can.

EUREKA AND THE TON OF BRICKS

Do you want to know something crazy? I didn't get really good at this consulting and coaching stuff until I became a mom.

Once I had kids, I found something more fulfilling than my career had ever been: raising good human beings, the kind you don't have to worry will turn into sociopaths when you aren't looking. Teaching my children to be empathetic, to want to help others, and to give something to the world—not just take from it—was simultaneously my biggest responsibility and my greatest joy. No pressure or anything.

My biggest professional "Eureka!" moment—the one with the proverbial ton of bricks—hit me when my then-nine-year-old son, Navin, was assigned to do a presentation about tornadoes to his class.

Navin had a checklist of project requirements and wanted to rush through his speech using exactly what would check the boxes. He wanted to use only the information that he was finding in his online sources. He was just going through the motions, so I said, "You can rush through and do exactly what the rubric says, and you'll probably get a good grade. That would be fine. Or, you can do what the checklist says *and* do something more, something the class would like. That will definitely get you a better grade, and the bonus is that the class will love your presentation."

It took a while for that thought to sink in. When it did, though, he created an interactive game loosely based on the old *$25,000 Pyramid.* As you would expect, everyone had a blast. No one else had done anything like it. He got an A+, and his teacher sent home a note saying, "Navin went so far above and beyond! He made sure that everyone was engaged and learned about tornadoes. I am very proud of him."

Navin was super-excited. He said to me, "Mom, I totally killed it. My presentation was beyond awesome."

After I rolled my eyes at his dramatic flair, I asked him "Do you understand why it was so good?"

"Yeah," he said, "I did more than I had to."

DO MORE THAN YOU HAVE TO

It was important to me that I hadn't told Navin what to do for his project. He had come up with his presentation himself. I did, though, help him shift his thinking in a way that helped him to really stand out.

The bricks hit me when I realized the way I'd worked with Navin in this situation was very similar to how I work with my sales professionals. The greatest success stories came not when I gave a sales rep exact direction or a checklist on what to do, but when I coached them on how to *think* through the sales situation and create ideas to make the customer's experience a remarkable one. This thought process ensured they would be able to exceed expectations and create confidence that would serve as momentum to continually accelerate their career.

Trying to make sure my kids make good choices, surpass expectations, and set themselves apart made me realize how incredible it would be if someone were to do the same for B2B sales professionals—for any employee, really. Coaching and enabling sales professionals is a journey that has culminated with this book. I have a genuine desire to help grow salespeople so they can take on the bots and the competition with confidence and ease.

It's not all that different in principle to how I approach being a mom.

I deliver personalized value by putting together who I am and how much I care to come up with ways to help my customers, the unique individuals, win in ways only they can. I've worked with—and loved—so many salespeople, and I want you all to succeed. This is 100 percent personal to me. I see tremendous value in what you do. And I have so much respect for this profession; it takes great courage to be able to deal with the level of rejection and negativity that you do on a daily basis. You deserve every success you achieve.

BECOME A PURVEYOR OF VALUE

Companies, speakers, and books will always have some sort of sales framework, checklist, or methodology that they tell reps to use. And the reality is that if you meticulously follow a methodology or go through and check all the boxes on a list, the likelihood of a sale may increase—but it still won't be a slam dunk. No checklist can guarantee differentiation. The fact that it is a checklist or methodology already implies it is being used by other sales professionals. So, if everyone is checking the same box to win a deal, there isn't room to be markedly different or better. In our hyper-competitive, uber-commoditized world, differentiating yourself in a way that creates unique value for your customers is the only way you'll win the big deals and create customers for life.

Because you bought this book, you are now one of my coaching clients. I may not have a weekly session scheduled with you, but this book is my way of being in your corner, trying to help you win. What I have shared with you throughout this book will help you achieve sustainable success in your career. You have kids to put through college, a new house to buy, and dozens of other responsibilities. The best way to reach these goals is by adopting the principle of personalized value.

Trust in who you are and what you stand for enough to know that you can create something uniquely valuable for your clients. Figure out what it's going to take to make your customer succeed, then make it happen. This will never be a one-size-fits-all process. Now that you have the thought process and mindset, I trust you to personalize in a way that makes each of your deals uniquely human-to-human.

Now, go out there and sell, using your heart and mind to reach your customers' hearts and minds. Go back and find opportunities to create personalized value. Test yourself against the critical questions you have learned. Be creative with your strategy for delivering personalized value, including when you will deliver it and how. Then, go make it a reality. The bots can't touch you because empathy-driven, trusted relationships cannot be automated or duplicated.

And know that if you do this, your own personal brand will emerge, one that is the exact opposite of Leisure Suit Larry. You will be a creator and purveyor of value. When you are genuine and become your customers' biggest advocate, they will become yours. That's how you create customers for life. Your loyal customers just won't want to buy from anyone, or anything, else.

Finally, as I have mentioned, coaches *live* for success stories. When you accelerate or win a deal based on something you have learned in this book, please let me know! Send me an e-mail at anielsen@ldkadvisory.com and tell me how you applied the thought process you learned here.

Someday, I want to be able to tell stories about *your* success to show other sales professionals how it's done!

APPENDIX

DISCOVERY QUESTIONS

Rider-Oriented Questions

What are the top business objectives for your organization this year?

What are some key initiatives aimed at helping achieve those business objectives?

How do you determine which business initiatives you will support?

What resources are required to execute on these initiatives?

What are your SLAs (service level agreements) and other key metrics?

What is working well, today? Why?

How do you allocate budget for your IT investments?

What types of information can we provide for you to help you make your decision?

Help me understand the current situation of {insert the specific context of your sale}.

Walk me through the process for {insert contextual information} today.

Elephant-Oriented Questions

If you had your way, a year from now you would be able to say, "I was a huge success last year because..."?

How do you feel the business perceives IT's role?

How do you address pressure from your leadership team to "innovate"?

Where do you see your career going at this company?

How can you make your team more successful?

What is your leadership expecting from you?

How do you want your team to be perceived? How about yourself?

How important is {insert initiative name} to your team? To you personally?

Looking out two years from now, what are your personal goals as it relates to your role within the organization?

Path-Related Questions

What risks do you anticipate with this change in technology?

What impact do you think an implementation effort would have on your end users?

Can you tell me about challenges with the implementation of technologies in the past?

What are your concerns around moving forward with our solution?

How do you feel the implementation process can be optimized?

Help me understand the role your team would play in a technology implementation. What do you believe their responsibilities will be?

What communication strategy do you use to inform your end-user community about an upcoming change, such as implementing this solution?

How could we, as your IT partner, help you feel confident about the implementation process?

To download a PDF of this page, please email
downloads@ldkadvisory.com.

THOUGHT PROCESS

Over time, with practice, you will get really good at thinking through the information you know about a customer and distilling the opportunities for you to create personalized value. Until then, though, walk through the following questions to help you uncover your opportunity for delivering personalized value for your customer in the context of your deal.

Based on what I have learned about the elephant in my customer discovery, what are the things that matter most to her, personally and professionally?

What can I do to help motivate the elephant? To address the pain that was uncovered in my discovery?

What are some things she enjoys doing? What are some things she has said she'd like to do one day—personally or professionally?

What could make her feel important? What could show her that she and her goals are important to me?

Is she facing any specific dysfunction in her role? Is there anything that I can do to help address that dysfunction?

What are my options for personalizing value, and which one will be the most impactful?

What can I do to make the buyer a hero?

Once you have some ideas for your options on personalized value, ask these questions:

Can anybody else do it?

Is this idea of personalized value creepy? Is it unethical?

How will my personalized value be perceived? Are there any "tests" I can do with the client to get a feel for what they may think if I deliver?

What's my best strategy for delivering personalized value to the right person?

What do I need to do to execute on this personalized value strategy?

How will I know if it mattered? What am I expecting?

If my value idea is perceived positively, are there follow-up activities I can do to ensure that the customer sees I am committed to their success, and that they don't feel like this is a "one and done" situation?

To download a PDF of this page, please email
downloads@ldkadvisory.com.

PRE-CALL PLANNING

Outcome: What is your desired outcome for this meeting? What is your Customer's desired outcome?

Set the Stage: How will you open the meeting? Draft the 1-2 sentence Introduction.

Desired Perception: How do you want the customer to perceive you, their sales professional?

Current Perception: How does the customer perceive you today?

Perception Management: What do you need to say and do, specifically, in this meeting to help shape the desired customer perception above?

Advance: What is the next step to advance the opportunity? What commitment do you need the customer to make by the end of this meeting?

To download a PDF of this page, please email
downloads@ldkadvisory.com.

PRE-CALL PLANNING, CONT'D

Direct RIDER: What does the "Rider" need to learn in this meeting for you to advance? What does the customer need to know in order to achieve the meeting's desired outcomes?

Motivate the ELEPHANT: What will you say to motivate the "Elephant" during this meeting so you can advance? What does the customer need to feel and believe in order to achieve the meeting's desired outcomes?

Shape the Path: In this meeting, how will you describe the path forward to the customer? Be sure to focus on how you will alleviate pains, eliminate obstacles, and mitigate any risks.

Messaging: What is the single most important and compelling message that needs to come across in this meeting? How will you ensure all your internal resources understand the message and align their talk tracks and comments?

To download a PDF of this page, please email
downloads@ldkadvisory.com.

BOOKS TO FEED YOUR BRAIN: RECOMMENDED READING

Some of these titles I have already referred to throughout this book; *all* have deeply impacted my approach to selling, training, and coaching. These are books that I believe every bot-beating sales professional needs to read. I trust that you'll find many ideas from these books that you will be able to apply to your sales motion to help you sell bigger, better, and more.

1. *Switch: How to Change Things When Change is Hard* by Chip and Dan Heath

2. *To Sell is Human: The Surprising Truth About Moving Others* by Daniel Pink

3. *Giftology: The Art and Science of Using Gifts to Cut Through the Noise, Increase Referrals, and Strengthen Retention* by John Ruhl

4. *Influence: The Psychology of Persuasion* by Robert Cialdini

5. *Give and Take: Why Helping Others Drives Our Success* by Adam Grant

6. *The Challenger Customer: Selling to the Hidden Influencer Who Can Multiply Your Results* by Brent Adamson, Matthew Dixon, Pat Spenner, and Nick Toman

7. *Mindset: The New Psychology of Success* by Carol S. Dweck

8. *Let's Get Real or Let's Not Play: Transforming the Buyer/Seller Relationship* by Mahan Khalsa and Randy Illig

9. *Never Split the Difference: Negotiating As If Your Life Depended On It* by Chris Voss

10. *The Like Switch: An Ex-FBI Agent's Guide to Influencing, Attracting, and Winning People Over* by Jack Schafer and Marvin Karlins

ACKNOWLEDGMENTS

For the past year or so, I have been making a list of people that have helped me get to where I am, today, and make this book a reality. Authoring this book is the most challenging thing I have ever done in my life (with the possible exception of childbirth, but I had an epidural, so it's a tough call). It has been exhilarating and exhausting to find the confidence and motivation to start the journey, to maintain that confidence throughout the frustrating, overwhelming process and, now, to have confidence enough to put this book out into the world knowing that some people just won't get it. There were so many times I was ready with a reason to quit. There were a few times that I was certain I was done. Luckily for me, I have always surrounded myself with people who don't let me give up. This book belongs to all of you, because without you it would still be a pipe dream.

Niyam, Navin & Marco—Thank you for your support and encouragement. Thank you for being either sounding board or guinea pig—whichever I needed, whenever I needed. Thank you for being the ones who made me realize that I am happiest when I know I have helped people grow and be their very best. Most of all, thank you for being OK with me having to miss out on some things so I could finish writing and achieve this crazy big goal. Kids, I hope that holding in your hands a book your mother wrote will make you realize that you can achieve great joy *and* success when you focus on helping others and put your heart and soul into doing something you are passionate about.

My Siblings—**Anil, Amita & Sunny**—Thanks for never letting me feel bad about not becoming a doctor and joining the medical field as you guys did. Words from each of your pep talks and encouragement over the years always helped push me forward when I got stuck. I am also pretty sure that if you guys would actually ever have really listened to my advice, I would not have been so hungry to find others who would, and eventually made a career out of coaching. So, thanks, I guess. *Hah.* Seriously, though, much of who

I am is a result of who you are and how much each of you means to me. I love you, big clowns.

Rajesh Dhawan—Thanks for being such an amazing big brother. I am forever grateful for your constant encouragement, steady support and always just being there when we need you. You are a rock for me and the entire family.

My Sweethearts—**Meher, Aanika & Sanya**, my nieces, and **Nihaal & Ajay**, my nephews. I can't wait to see the amazing things each of you will do and be. I hope this book shows you to always chase your crazy big goals because if you put your heart and minds to it, you will achieve them.

Sonal Gupta—I am so grateful to have you in my life. There's no way I will come up with words to explain how much you and your constant support mean to me. For every time I got stuck in this writing process, you unstuck me and reminded me that I have what it takes to achieve this goal. I lost track of how many times you pulled me out of the pit of quicksand that my nervous mind manufactured. I am thankful to you for being my person and unconditionally standing in my corner ready to cheer, be a shoulder to cry on or to give me a kick in the ass. Most of all, thank you for being the one person who knows exactly which of these things I need, every single time.

Jamie Lee—Thank you for helping me gain confidence in my knowledge and expertise, particularly with Psych2Sell. I appreciate the many incredible opportunities you've given me to help your sales team learn and grow. The chance to make a difference in their lives by helping them be the best sales professionals they can is something I never take for granted. Watching the account managers win when they adopted what I taught and coached has been the fuel that helped get this elephant moving on the right path. This is what ultimately gave me the courage to write this book. Working with you in support of the sales organization has been a complete blast. You are an inspiring leader and your genuine care and concern for your people is something I wish every sales leader would learn.

Mark Wechsler—If there was any doubt before about how much of an impact your leadership had on me, I hope this acknowledgment clears it up. Thanks so much, Mark, for taking a chance on me. I will never forget what you said to me when you called with the job offer: "I interviewed people with more experience, but I don't think I've ever interviewed anyone with your enthusiasm and hunger. That will make you the most successful one on the team." It was the first role where I was able to excel at sales support and leading large deal pursuit efforts. What I learned during that time is priceless. I can't imagine how I would have gotten to writing this book had you not put me in the trenches with so many sales professionals to learn what personalized value is and what it is not.

Bob Hollander—Thank you for being my first customer and one of my biggest champions. Your faith in me and my contribution to sales success is something I will always be grateful for. Before you tapped me to join your Sales Enablement team, I barely knew what that entailed. Thanks for that opportunity. It was a big part of how I got here.

Minoo Jalal—There are few people I have met that have the integrity you do. Your constant motivation to do the right thing and help others do things right is inspiring. It has been a complete joy to work with you and watch you grow so much in areas that you somehow didn't believe you could or would. Not only that, but I owe much of my confidence in what I do for my clients to your honest feedback and consistent support. Thank you for letting me be a small part of your growth journey, and please know that you have helped me so much in mine, too.

Tucker Max—I learned more about my writing and how to turn my ideas into a book from your two-day Guided Author workshop than I did in all the previous years I had considered being an author. Your sincere desire to see authors succeed was inspiring and your words of advice helped give me the confidence to actually move forward and make this book a reality.

James Timberlake—I don't know how many times you talked me off a ledge throughout the process of writing this book. I cannot thank you enough for keeping me sane during one of the most challenging experiences I have ever been through. I am grateful to you for your time and encouragement and for being my advocate over the past year. There would not even be a book without your consistent support and encouragement.

Meghan McCracken—I cannot thank you enough for the meticulous editing you have done for this book. Your patience with me and all the additions and changes I have made over the past several months has been incredible. Thank you for helping me get back on track after the process fell apart; I could not be happier that I have had the opportunity to work with and learn from such a talented writer and editor.

Lisa Sass—You are one of the most creative and inspiring people I have ever met. I am grateful for your support and encouragement when I needed it the most. When I first went out on my own and my confidence was low, your cheerleading helped me to keep my head on straight, stay true to myself and have faith that you can be successful when you do what you love. I can always count on you to make me laugh and I am blessed to call you a friend.

Jo Anne Myers—You are an amazing coach and I am grateful that I have you to guide me. You've managed to help build my confidence a great deal over the past several months and I tell you, that is no small feat! It is such a joy to work with you and I continue to grow because of it.

Sheila Coffman—I will never forget your support and encouragement when I was in a situation where my self-serving boss wanted me to sell you on ideas that were of no value to you. If you wouldn't have had the faith in me that you did, I doubt that I would have left that narcissistic, egomaniacal boss when I did and had the courage to go out on my own. Thank you for your friendship, coaching, and support as I reminded myself who I am, what I stand for and that I can never compromise when it comes to creating personalized value for my clients.

To the thought leaders and mentors who have so generously helped educate and guide me in my field of sales performance coaching and enablement: the content you have shared and the conversations I have had with you over the past few years have had a tremendous impact on me and my success. I am grateful for your generosity in sharing your knowledge or time with me. Some of you I've had the pleasure of meeting, and others, I hope to meet one day. Thank you, Mike Kunkle, Lori Richardson, Alice Heiman, Trish Bertuzzi, Jim Ninnivagi, Deb Calvert, Tim Riesterer, Tamara Schenk, Gerhard Gschwandtner, Jill Konrath, and Jill Rowley.

My beloved B2B sales professionals without whom I would not be able to live my "why." Thank you for letting me be a part of your journey, listening to my nagging guidance and applying it to help you grow. I live for the calls that come after you have used some psychology to help you with a customer. It never gets old to hear, "Dude, you were right, it totally worked!" There's no way I can list all of the wonderful sales professionals I have to thank for my success, but a few of my favorites from over the years are easy to call out. Here goes...

Mike Winkelmann, Antonio Leon, Joe Watson, Saam Fouladgar, Juan Carlos Anzola, Jeff Miller, Chris Campbell, Ben Burnett, Melanie Wise, Phil Rutland, Scott Moore, Joe Phelps, Tony Marcozzi, Steve Zaehler, Jenna Timp, Nick Loredo, Steve Klonsky, Sandy Quinn, Hannah Rott, Kory Casto, Mark Thomas, Bailey Swartz, Geoff Adams, Mason

Sherman, Bruce Keating, Ray Panice, Ryan McCarthy, Kelly Lynch, Dave Unger, Steve Bochenski, Nick Anderson, and Mooky Desai.

Thank you to the sales, engineering and other senior business leaders with whom I have worked and helped improve organizational health, increase revenue, and improve sales engagement. I appreciate you for listening so carefully to my guidance and taking action on my recommendations, even when they felt "soft." Thank you for understanding how important it is to put humans first, care for sales and marketing professionals, and do what it takes to help them achieve their potential. Thank you to Richard Dresden, Tom Van Sickle, Robert Kirk, Steve Garrou, Mike Camacho, Kevin Barker, Jeff Ton, Charles Jones, Vic Tingler, Jim Leake, James Bernal, Walt Strubbe, Jeff Olson, Vijay Motiramani, Scott Eidle, Mandy Cozby, Alicia Gaba, Jennifer Vogel, David Snyder, Pat Spencer, Tom Holt, Steve Busselman, Jon Shende, Ron Schmidt, Jessica Morin, Noor Lodhi, Michelle Genser, Twann Atkins, and John Barrar.

Lastly, and probably the most important of all, I'd like to thank Janet Look, my senior-year high school English teacher, for helping me recognize my love for writing.

ABOUT THE AUTHOR

Anita Nielsen is a Sales Performance Consultant, coach, blogger, and thought leader with over twenty years of experience in B2B sales and support, primarily focused on technology product and solution providers.

Her company, LDK Advisory Services, LLC. was founded in 2014 and works with B2B sales organizations of all sizes and across industries to help develop sales enablement strategies, programs, content, and collateral, and provide coaching to sales professionals and sales leaders.

Anita is devoted to helping sales professionals understand the basics of psychology and human behavior and apply them in consultative sales interactions to win bigger, better, and more. Her proprietary Psych2Sell training is growing in popularity amongst B2B sales organizations and has been called the "secret sauce" for developing high-performing, future-ready B2B sales professionals.

Recognized as one of *Selling Power Magazine*'s Top Sales Enablement Consultants of 2018, Anita works with sales professionals, teaching them how to create differentiating value that enables them to supersize commission checks and accelerate organizational growth. Anita also donates her time to coach and guide women with careers in technology and sales. Anita is a strong advocate for growing and developing high-performing sales professionals through personalized training and coaching.

Anita attended the University of Illinois to attain her bachelor's degree in psychology and the New York Institute of Technology for her master's in business administration with a focus on leadership.

Anita was born in Punjab, India and her parents moved the family to the United States when she was two years old. Currently, she lives in Chicagoland with her husband, Marco, and two teenaged children, Niyam and Navin. She loves to cook, is a podcast junkie, and may be a professional binge-watcher. Currently, she is trying to survive her children's adolescent years without going completely grey or succumbing to overwhelming Tiger Mom urges.

Made in the USA
Lexington, KY
21 June 2019